W9-BTD-008

WITHDRAWAL

POLITICAL WORKS
OF CONCEALED AUTHORSHIP

THE

POLITICKS

And VIEWS

Of a Certain

PARTY,

DISPLAYED.

Printed in the Year M,DCC,XCII.

Attributed to William Loughton Smith. No. 92-22.
(The "Certain Party" was Thomas Jefferson)

POLITICAL WORKS
OF CONCEALED AUTHORSHIP
RELATING TO THE UNITED STATES
1789-1810
WITH ATTRIBUTIONS

Compiled by
PIERCE WELCH GAINES

THIRD EDITION
REVISED AND ENLARGED

THE SHOE STRING PRESS, INC.
HAMDEN, CONNECTICUT
1972

Library of Congress Cataloging in Publication Data

Gaines, Pierce Welch.
    Political works of concealed authorship relating
to the United States, 1789-1810.

    First published in 1959 under title: Political
works of concealed authorship during the administrations of Washington, Adams, and Jefferson, 1789-
1809.
    1. Anonyms and pseudonyms, American. 2. U. S.
--Politics and government--Constitutional period,
1789-1809--Bibliography. I. Title.
Z1045.G3 1972   016.3209'73'04   76-178861
ISBN 0-208-01241-9

Printed in the United States of America

CONTENTS

ILLUSTRATIONS

INTRODUCTION

Who needs it, this book I mean? In recent years so much
has been done to facilitate identification of the authors of
anonymous (including pseudonymous) early American works.
For the Evans period through 1800 there is the Bristol author
and title index, and very recently we have had the Short Title
Evans, which lists titles and authors and adds some 10,000
works "not in Evans", and Bristol's Supplement to Evans,
which adds some 1200 more. For 1801 through 1810 the
Shaw and Shoemaker volumes now have a title index and an
author index. For works not published in this country reliance
is still owed to Sabin, which is considerably out of date. A
chronological computer printout by the John Carter Brown
Library correlating Sabin entries now permits a check of
duplicate listings so as to find hidden attributions.

Yet withal there frequently is no short and easy way to the
identification of authors of anonymous works. For one thing
authorities have difficulty keeping up with late particulars.
New biographies, histories, &c. continue to record new facts.
Also it must be said that the big general works are difficult to
keep in close control. In the Short Title Evans, for example, a
check showed more than forty cases in the period 1789-1800
where no attribution was made although made here, or where
the attribution was different from that suggested here, or
where there was no entry. Over forty other cases were noted
where attributions were made but the titles did not appear in
the alphabetical sequence.

Within its limits (which include fewer years than one could
wish) this compilation will provide useful information, I think,
which in many instances cannot readily be found anywhere
else. Conversely, if a title does not appear here, it will be very

difficult to find the name of the author in any other source.
A total of one hundred and forty sources are cited here.

The present volume is a revision and enlargement of a work
completed in 1964, which itself replaced an earlier version
completed in 1958. There are 941 titles in this volume, 294
more than in its immediate predecessor, and many prior
entries have been revised and enlarged.

Included now are summaries of the entries from my work
on William Cobbett, the prolific pro-English pamphleteer who
enlivened the scene at Philadelphia when it was the national
capital. (The work is listed under "Gaines" in the "Sources of
the Attributions" which follow.) These entries disclose the
considerable number of editions, &c., which have not hereto-
fore been generally known.

The year-by-year method of presentation is used as provid-
ing the most ready reference and as presenting each work in
its contemporary setting. To take care of the cases where the
date of the work is attributed, a separate short-title listing of
such works is included. In the alphabetical arrangement the
initial "a", "an" and "the" have been disregarded. The sources
of the attributions are usually abbreviated, and the full titles
may be found in the "Sources of the Attributions" in the
pages immediately following. Explanatory comment will indi-
cate the view expressed in any source which differs from the
attribution given. Sources are cited which seem to constitute
adequate precedent or which otherwise might be particularly
helpful, such as the Dictionary of American Biography and
the Catalogue of the Library of Thomas Jefferson, prepared
by Millicent Sowerby.

The brief descriptions of the works listed are not based on
an examination of all the works themselves. Matter omitted
is indicated by . . . , and there is no attempt to include all the
original capitalization and punctuation. A date in parentheses
indicates that the date is supplied. References to the sources

are to the number assigned, if any, or otherwise to the page indicated.

Over the years in connection with preparation of the *Political Works,* and its corrections and additions, assistance and encouragement have been received for which I would like to express grateful appreciation to Messrs. Julian P. Boyd, Roger P. Bristol, L. H. Butterfield, Richard Beale Davis, Robert E. Moody, Cedric L. Robinson, Clifford K. Shipton, Michael J. Walsh, Edwin Wolf, 2nd, and to Mr. and Mrs. Edmund Berkeley. I salute also the memories of James T. Babb, Clarence S. Brigham, John Ottemiller and R. W. G. Vail.

Fairfield, Connecticut   P. W. G.
February 23, 1971.

SOURCES OF THE ATTRIBUTIONS

Abernethy
The South in the New Nation 1789-1819. Thomas P. Abernethy. Baton Rouge, Louisiana State University Press, 1961.

A.I.I.
American Imprints Inventory. 5: Kentucky Imprints 1787-1810, Louisville, Historical records survey, 1939; 9: New Jersey Imprints 1784-1800, Baltimore, WPA Historical records survey project, 1939; 40: Massachusetts Imprints 1801, Boston, American imprints inventory project, 1942.

Alden
Rhode Island Imprints 1727-1800. John Eliot Alden. New York, for the Bibliographical Society of America [by] Bowker, 1949.

Ap. Cyc.
Appleton's Cyclopaedia of American Biography. New York, D. Appleton and Company 1887-89. 6 vols.

Austin
Early American Medical Imprints . . . 1668-1820. Robert B. Austin. Washington, U.S. Government Printing Office, 1961.

B.A.L.
Bibliography of American Literature. Jacob Blanck. 4 vols. New Haven, Yale University Press, 1955-

Baker
Bibliotheca Washingtoniana. W. S. Baker. Philadelphia, Robert M. Lindsay, 1889.

Baldwin
Life and Letters of Simeon Baldwin. Simeon E. Baldwin. New Haven, Tuttle, Morehouse & Taylor, 1919.

Bartlett
A Catalogue of Books . . . in the Library of John Carter Brown . . . Part III, Vol. II. John Russell Bartlett. New York, Kraus Reprint Corporation, 1963.

B. Ath.
Catalogue of the Washington Collection in the Boston Athenaeum. Appleton P. C. Griffin. Boston, The Boston Athenaeum, 1897.

Beard
Economic Origins of Jeffersonian Democracy. Charles A. Beard. New York, The Macmillan Company, 1936.

Bemis   American Secretaries of State and their diplomacy.
                         Samuel Flagg Bemis, editor. Vol. III. New
                         York, Alfred A. Knopf, 1927.
Boyd   The Papers of Thomas Jefferson, Julian P. Boyd,
                         Editor. Princeton University Press. In process.
Brant   James Madison, 1787-1800; do. 1800-1809. Irving
                         Brant. Indianapolis, The Bobbs-Merrill Company,
                         1950, 1953.
Brin.   Catalogue of the Library of George Brinley (at auc-
                         tion). Hartford, Case, Lockwood & Brainard
                         Company, 1878-1891.
Bristol   Maryland Imprints 1801-1810. Roger P. Bristol.
                         Charlottesville, by the University of Virginia
                         Press, 1953.
Bryan   George Washington in American Literature 1775-
                         1865. William Alfred Bryan. New York, Colum-
                         bia University Press, 1952.
Church   Library of E. D. Church. George Watson Cole. 5
                         vols. New York, Dodd, Mead and Co., 1907.
CHA   Dictionary Catalogue of the History of the Americas.
                         The New York Public Library. 28 vols. Boston,
                         G. K. Hall & Co., 1961.
Clark   Peter Porcupine in America, 1792-1800. Mary E.
                         Clark. Philadelphia, 1939.
Clark, ed.   Travels in the Old South. Edited by Thomas D.
                         Clark. 2 vols. Norman, University of Oklahoma
                         Press, 1956.
Cobbett   Letters from William Cobbett to Edward Thornton
                         . . . Edited by G. D. H. Cole. London, Oxford
                         University Press, 1937.
Cooley   Vermont Imprints before 1800. Elizabeth F.
                         Cooley. Montpelier, Vermont Historical Society,
                         1937.
Cronin &   A Bibliography of John Adams and John Quincy
   Wise Adams   Adams. John W. Cronin and W. Harvey Wise, Jr.
                         Washington, Riverford Publishing Company,
                         1935. John Adams section.
Cronin & Wise   Same. John Quincy Adams section.
   J. Q. Adams
Cronin & Wise   A Bibliography of James Madison and James Mon-
   Madison   roe. John W. Cronin and W. Harvey Wise, Jr.
                         1935. Madison section.

Cronin & Wise Monroe	Same. Monroe section.
Cunningham	The Jeffersonian Republicans in Power. Noble E. Cunningham, Jr. Chapel Hill, University of North Carolina Press. 1963.
Cush.	Initials and Pseudonyms. William Cushing. 1st, 2nd Ser. New York, T. Y. Crowell & Co., 1885, 1888.
D.A.B.	Dictionary of American Biography. New York, Charles Scribner's Sons, 1958. 20 vols. in 10.
Dauer	The Adams Federalists. Manning J. Dauer. Baltimore, Johns Hopkins Press, 1953.
Davis	Intellectual Life in Jefferson's Virginia. Richard Beale Davis. Chapel Hill, University of North Carolina Press, 1964.
Dex.	Biographical Sketches of the Graduates of Yale College. Franklin B. Dexter. 3rd-5th Ser. New York, H. Holt and Company, 1903-1911.
Dumbauld	Thomas Jefferson American Tourist. Edward Dumbauld. Norman, University of Oklahoma Press, 1946.
DuPuy	Library of Henry F. DuPuy. New York. Anderson Galleries, 1919, 1920.
Edinburgh	Catalogue of the Printed Books in the Library of the University of Edinburgh. University Press, Edinburgh, 3 vols., 1918-1923.
E.	American Bibliography. Charles Evans. Vols. 7-13. Chicago, for the author, 1912-55.
E. Supp.	Supplement to Charles Evans' American Bibliography. Roger P. Bristol. Charlottesville, University Press of Virginia, 1970.
Finotti	Bibliographia Catholica Americana. Part I. Joseph M. Finotti. New York, The Catholic Publication House, 1872.
Fisher	The Publications of Thomas Collier 1784-1808. Samuel H. Fisher. Litchfield, Litchfield Historical Society, 1933.
Ford	Bibliotheca Hamiltoniana. Paul L. Ford. New York, for the author, The Knickerbocker Press, 1886.
Gaines	William Cobbett and the United States 1792-1835. Pierce W. Gaines. Worcester, American Antiquarian Society, 1971.

Gilman   Bibliography of Vermont. M. D. Gilman. Burling-
                       ton, Free Press Association, 1897.
Halk.   Dictionary of Anonymous and Pseudonymous En-
                       glish Literature. Halkett and Laing. New ed.
                       Edinburgh, Oliver and Boyd, 1926-1934.
Hamilton Papers   The Papers of Alexander Hamilton. New York,
                       Columbia University Press, 1961- .
Hammond   The History of Political Parties in the State of New
                       York. Jabez D. Hammond. Third edition. Vol
                       1. Cooperstown, H. & E. Phinney, 1845.
Harrison   John Breckinridge, Jeffersonian Republican.
                       Lowell H. Harrison. Louisville, Filson Club,
                       1969.
Higginbotham   The Keystone in the Democratic Arch: Pennsyl-
                       vania Politics 1800-1816. Sanford W. Higgin-
                       botham. Harrisburg, Pa. Hist. and Mus. Comm.,
                       1952.
Hill   American Plays, 1714-1830. Frank P. Hill. Stan-
                       ford, Stanford University Press, 1934.
Howard   The Connecticut Wits. Leon Howard. Chicago,
                       University of Chicago Press (1943).
Howes   U.S.—IANA (1650-1950). Wright Howes. New
                       York, Bowker, 1962.
Jacobs   Tarnished Warrior Major-General James Wilkinson.
                       James R. Jacobs. New York, The Macmillan
                       Company, 1938.
Jeff.   Catalogue of the Library of Thomas Jefferson. E.
                       Millicent Sowerby. 5 vols. Washington (U.S.)
                       Government Printing Office, 1952-1959.
Jillson   Rare Kentucky Books. Willard Jillson. Louisville,
                       Standard Printing Co., 1939.
Johnston   Contribution to a bibliography of Thomas Jeffer-
                       son. Richard H. Johnston. Washington, Thomas
                       Jefferson Memorial Association, 1904.
Kress   The Kress Library of Business and Economics.
                       Catalogue 1777-1817 and Supplement 1473-
                       1848. Boston, Harvard Graduate School of Busi-
                       ness Administration, 1957, 1967.
LCP   Catalogue of the Books . . . Library Company of
                       Philadelphia. Philadelphia, C. Sherman & Co.,
                       1835.

McCorison	Vermont Imprints 1778-1820. Marcus A. McCorison. Worcester, American Antiquarian Society, 1963.
McLean	George Tucker . . . Robert Colin McLean. Chapel Hill, University of North Carolina Press, 1961.
McMurtrie	A Bibliography of Mississippi Imprints 1798-1830. Douglas C. McMurtrie. Beauvoir community, The Book Farm, 1945.
Malone	Jefferson and his Time. Dumas Malone. Boston, Little, Brown, 1951- .
Minick	A History of Printing in Maryland 1791-1800. A. Rachel Minick. Baltimore, Enoch Pratt Free Library, 1949.
Mitchell	Alexander Hamilton. The National Adventure 1788-1804. Broadus Mitchell. New York, The Macmillan Company, 1962.
Monaghan	French Travellers in the United States 1765-1932. Frank Monaghan. Supplement by Samuel J. Marino. New York, Antiquarian Press Ltd., 1961.
Morison	Harrison Gray Otis. Samuel Eliot Morison. Boston, Houghton Mifflin Company, 1969.
Morse	The Federalist Party in Massachusetts to the Year 1800. Anson Ely Morse. Princeton, The University Library, 1909.
Mott	A History of American Magazines 1741-1850. Frank L. Mott. Cambridge, Harvard University Press, 1957.
Nichols	Bibliography of Worcester . . . 1775-1848. C. L. Nichols. 2d. ed. Worcester, Priv. print., 1918.
Noyes	A Bibliography of Maine Imprints to 1820. R. Webb Noyes. Stonington, 1930.
NYHS	Catalogue of the . . . library of the New York Historical Society (Reverend Timothy Alden). New York, J. Seymour, 1813.
NYPL	Checklist of Additions to Evans' American Bibliography . . . New York Public Library . . . Lewis M. Stark and Maud D. Cole, 1960.
Palmer	The Age of the Democratic Revolution . . . The Struggle. R. R. Palmer. Princeton, Princeton University Press, 1964.

Paltsits	A Bibliography of . . . Philip Freneau. Victor Hugo Paltsits. New York, Dodd, Mead and Company, 1903.
Pearl	William Cobbett. M. L. Pearl. London, Oxford University Press, 1953.
Plumer	Life of William Plumer. William Plumer Junior. Boston, Phillips Sampson and Co., 1856.
Purcell	Connecticut in Transition 1775-1818. Richard J. Purcell. Washington, American Historical Association, 1918.
Quinn	A History of the American Drama from the Beginning to the Civil War. Arthur Hobson Quinn. New York, 1923.
Reed	A Bibliography of Delaware through 1960. H. Clay Reed and Marion B. Reed. Newark, University of Delaware Press, 1966.
Rich	Bibliotheca Americana Nova. Obadiah Rich. 3 vols. London, O. Rich, 1835-1844.
Roberts	Moreau de St. Méry's American Journey. Kenneth Roberts, ed. Garden City, Doubleday & Company, 1947.
Rogers	Evolution of a Federalist. William Loughton Smith . . . George C. Rogers, Junior. Columbia, University of South Carolina Press, 1962.
Rowe	Mathew Carey. Kenneth W. Rowe. Baltimore, The Johns Hopkins Press, 1933.
S.	Dictionary of Books Relating to America. Joseph Sabin. 29 vols. New York, J. Sabin, 1868-1936.
Servies	A Bibliography of John Marshall. James A. Servies. Washington, U.S. Government Printing Office, 1956.
Shaw	American Bibliography, a Preliminary Checklist for 1801 (-1810). Compiled by Ralph R. Shaw and Richard H. Shoemaker. New York, The Scarecrow Press, Inc., 1958, 1961. 10 vols.
Sibley	Sibley's Harvard Graduates. Vol. XIV. Clifford K. Shipton. Boston, Massachusetts Historical Society, 1968.
Simms	Life of John Taylor. Henry H. Simms. Richmond, William Byrd Press, 1932.
Skeel	A Bibliography of the Writings of Noah Webster. Emily E. F. Skeel. New York, New York Public Library, 1958.

SOURCES OF THE ATTRIBUTIONS

Smith	Freedom's Fetters. James M. Smith. Ithaca, Cornell University Press, 1956.
Smith, P.	John Adams. Page Smith. 2 vols. Garden City, Doubleday & Company, Inc., 1962.
Spargo	Anthony Haswell. John Spargo. Rutland, The Tuttle Company, 1925.
STE	National Index of American Imprints through 1800. The Short-Title Evans. 2 vols. Worcester, American Antiquarian Society, 1969.
Stillwell	Washington Eulogies . . . Margaret Bingham Stillwell. New York Public Library, 1916.
Streeter	The Celebrated Collection . . . Thomas Winthrop Streeter . . . Vols. 2 and 3. Parke-Bernet Galleries Inc., New York, 1967, 1968.
Swem	A Bibliography of Virginia. Parts I and II. Earl G. Swem. Richmond, Virginia State Library, 1916.
Tapley	Salem Imprints 1768-1825. Harriet S. Tapley. Salem, The Essex Institute, 1927.
Tolles	George Logan of Philadelphia. Frederick B. Tolles. New York, Oxford University Press, 1953.
Tompk. Burr	Burr Bibliography. Hamilton B. Tompkins. Brooklyn, Historical Printing Club, 1892.
Tompk. Jeff.	Bibliotheca Jeffersoniana. Hamilton B. Tompkins. New York, G. P. Putnam's Sons, 1887.
Trumb.	List of Books Printed in Connecticut 1709-1800. James Hammond Trumbull. Hartford, Case, Lockwood & Brainard Company, 1904. Supp. Hartford, Acorn Club, 1938, 1947.
Turnbull	Bibliography of South Carolina. Vol. 1. Robert J. Turnbull. Charlottesville, University of Virginia Press, 1956.
Turner	William Plumer of New Hampshire 1759-1850. Lynn W. Turner. Chapel Hill, University of North Carolina Press, 1962.
Vail	The Voice of the Old Frontier. R. W. G. Vail. Philadelphia, University of Pennsylvania Press, 1949.
Walters	Alexander James Dallas. Raymond Walters, Jr. Philadelphia, University of Pennsylvania Press, 1943.
Wandell	Aaron Burr in Literature. Samuel H. Wandell. London, K. Paul, Trench, Trubner & Co., 1936.

Weg.   Early American Poetry. Oscar Wegelin. New York,
                        P. Smith, 1930.
Wheat   Maps and Charts Published in America Before 1800.
                        James C. Wheat, Christian F. Brun. New Haven,
                        Yale University Press, 1969.
Wheaton   Some Account . . . Life . . . of William Pinkney.
                        Henry Wheaton. New York, J. W. Palmer & Co.,
                        1826.
Wise & Cronin   A Bibliography of Thomas Jefferson. W. H. Wise,
                        Jr. and J. W. Cronin, Washington, Riverford Pub-
                        lishing Company, 1935.
Wolfe   Jeffersonian Democracy in South Carolina. John
                        H. Wolfe. Chapel Hill, University of North Caro-
                        lina Press, 1940.

SOME OTHER SOURCES EXAMINED

American Imprints Inventory: Chicago, The WPA historical records survey project:
- 12 Sag Harbor, L.I. 1791-1820. 1939.
- 14 West Virginia. 1791-1830. 1940.
- 16 Tennessee. 1793-1840. Nashville, Tennessee historical records survey, 1941.
- 17 Ohio. 1796-1820. Columbus, Ohio historical records survey, 1942.
- 32 Tennessee. 1793-1840. 1942.
- 36 Utica, N.Y. 1799-1830. 1942.
- 38 Kentucky. 1788-1820. Louisville, historical records survey, 1942.
- 45 Massachusetts. 1802. Boston, historical records survey, 1942.

DeRenne, Wymberley Jones (Library of). Books Relating to . . . Georgia. [Branch, The Morning news, 1911]. 1905.

Ford, Paul L. The Journals of Hugh Gaine, Printer. Vol. 1. N.Y., Dodd, Mead & Company, 1902.

Ford, Worthington C. Broadsides . . . Massachusetts. 1639-1800. Boston, Massachusetts Historical Society, 1922.

Gilmore, Barbara. A Puritan Town and its Imprints. Northampton 1786-1845. Northampton, Hampshire bookshop, 1942.

Hill, F. P. and Collins, V. L. Books . . . Newark, New Jersey. 1775-1900. Newark [Courier-Citizen Company], 1902.

McMurtrie, Douglas C.:
- A Bibliography of Morristown Imprints 1798-1820. Newark, Priv. print., 1936.
- Checklist of Books . . . Schenectady, N.Y. 1795-1830. Chicago, 1938.
- Early Printing in Michigan 1796-1850. Chicago, John Calhoun Club, 1931.

Early Printing in New Orleans. New Orleans, Searen & Platt, Ltd., 1929.

Early Printing in Tennessee 1793-1830. Chicago, Chicago club of printing house craftsmen, 1933.

Eighteenth Century North Carolina Imprints 1749-1800. Chapel Hill, University of North Carolina Press, 1938.

Louisiana Imprints 1768-1810. Hattiesburg, The Book Farm, 1942.

Maine Imprints 1792-1820. Chicago, Priv. print., 1935.

Nelson, William. Checklist of the Issues of the Press of New Jersey to 1800. Paterson, Call Printing and Publishing Co., 1899.

Paine, N. List of Early American Broadsides . . . Worcester, C. Hamilton, 1897.

Perrin, William H. The Pioneer Press of Kentucky. 1787-1830. [Louisville] J. P. Morton & Co., 1888.

Sealock, Richard B. and Seeley, Pauline A. Long Island Bibliography. Baltimore [Ann Arbor, Edwards Brothers], 1940.

Sears, Joseph H. Tennessee Printers 1791-1945. Kingsport, Kingsport Press, 1945.

Thompson, Donald E. A Bibliography of Louisiana Books and Pamphlets. University of Alabama Press, 1947.

Waters, Willard O. American Imprints 1648-1797 in the Huntington Library. Cambridge, 1933.

Weeks, Stephen B. Press of North Carolina in the Eighteenth Century. Brooklyn, Historical Printing Club, 1891.

Wheeler, Joseph T. The Maryland Press 1777-1790. Baltimore, Maryland Historical Society, 1938.

POLITICAL WORKS

OF CONCEALED AUTHORSHIP

WORKS OF CONCEALED AUTHORSHIP

1789

89-01   Attention! or, New thoughts on a serious subject; . . . Excise laws of Connecticut . . . By a Private Citizen. Hartford . . . 1789. 8vo. 18p.

By Noah Webster, Jr.

E. 22258; S. 102339; Trumb. 1593; Dex. 4p. 71; Skeel 719.

89-02   The Dangerous vice . . . A fragment . . . By a Gentleman Formerly of Boston . . . Columbia printed. 1789. 8vo. 16p.

By Edward Church.

E. 21736; S. 12986; Sibley 14: 392,3. E. says also attr. Silvanus Bourne. Sibley says the "vice" was John Adams. See Smith, P., Vol. 2, pp. 778,9.

89-03   Decius's Letters on the opposition to the new constitution in Virginia, 1789. Richmond. 8vo. (2)134p.

By James Montgomery or John Nicholas, Jr.

E. 21971; S. 100451; CHA 15987 3: 1; Jeff. 3152; Howes M. 742 have Montgomery. John Adams attr. to John Nicholas. Jefferson attr. dedication to Nicholas and rest to Montgomery. Also S. 50137. A third edition is attributed to Nicholas in S. 55169 (Never published?). Nicholas preferred in Boyd, Vol. 16, p. 141, in a detailed discussion.

89-04   Description du sol, des productions . . . portion des Etats-Unis. . . . Paris, 1789. 8vo. 30p.

By Manasseh Cutler.

CHA 6037 1: 3; S. 18176.

89-05   A dissertation on the manner of acquiring the character . . . of
          a citizen of the United States. . . . 1789. 8vo. 8p.

          By David Ramsey.

          E. 22088; S. 67684.

89-06   An essay on the seat of the federal government . . . delicate
          morals . . . in infant states . . . By a Citizen of Philadelphia.
          . . . Philadelphia . . . 1789. 8vo. (2)34p.

          By Pelatiah Webster.

          E. 22262; S. 102411; Howes W209.

89-07   Examen du gouvernement d'Angleterre, comparé aux constitu-
          tions des États-Unis. . . . London 1789. 8vo. viii, 291p.

          By John Stevens.

          CHA 6899 1:3; Jeff. 3003; Howes S968; S. 91540+.
          Attributed also to William Livingston S. 41646; E. 20465
          (1787 edition); Bartlett 3294.

89-08   Observations on the agriculture, manufactures and commerce
          of the United States. . . . By a Citizen of the United States.
          New York . . . 1789. 8vo. 102p.

          By Tench Coxe.

          E. 21774; S. 17301; Jeff. 3627.

89-09   Observations on the propriety of fixing . . . permanent residence
          of Congress. . . . (New York) 1789. Signed, Phocion. 8vo.
          11p.

          By Thomas Hartley.

          E. 21878; S. 30697.

89-10   Ode to be sung on the arrival of the President . . . (New York
          1789). Broadside.

          By Samuel Low.

          STE 45505; E. Supp. B6974.

89-11   Ode to the president of the United States on his arrival at
         Boston. (Boston 1789). Broadside.

         By Oliver Holden.

         STE 45496. E. Supp. B7018 not attr.

89-12   On monies, coins, weights, and measures proposed for the
         United States. . . . Philadelphia . . . 1789. Signed "B". 8vo.
         (2)25(1)p; illus.

         By John Beale Bordley.

         Kress S. 5212; S. 93803+; Boyd, Vol. 16, p. 603; E. 21698.
         S. 57275 not attr.

89-13   The political passing bell. Written in a country meeting house
         . . . in the true spirit of party. . . . Boston . . . 1789. 8vo.
         15p.

         By George Richards.

         STE 22116; Weg. 328. S. 63794 not attributed.

89-14   The politician outwitted. A comedy . . . By an American. . . .
         New York . . . 1789. 8vo. 71p.

         By Samuel Low.

         E. 21926; S. 42405; Hill 170; Weg. p. 55.

89-15   A Private citizen begs leave humbly to submit the following
         queries to . . . General Assembly now sitting, . . . (1789).
         Fol. Broadside.

         By George Mason.

         E. 21941.

89-16   Purport of a letter on sheep. . . . Maryland . . . 1789. Caption
         title. 8vo. 6p. Signed "B".

         By John Beale Bordley.

         E. 21699.

89-17   A short representation . . . trade with the United States of

America. . . . London . . . 1789. 32p; also 26p., front.; also title omits "the United States of", 32p.

By Patrick Colquhoun?

Kress B. 1720 (not attr.) and Kress S. 5226 (26p.). Sabin 80681,82 (each 32p., not attr.).

89-18 To the electors at the ensuing election. Fellow citizens, as I am a candidate for office . . . A Planter. (Savannah, 1789). Broadside.

By Samuel Chandler.

E.21732; S. 95917. See no. 89-20.

89-19 To the independent and patriotic electors of the State of New York. . . . (New York, April 1, 1789). 8vo. 12p.

By Alexander Hamilton.

E. 21872; Hamilton Papers V pp. 310-315.

89-20 To the public. With astonishment I read a late publication . . . by one Samuel Chandler . . . Philalathes. (Savannah 1789). Broadside.

By Robert Montfort.

E. 21970. See no. 89-18.

89-21 To the supervisors of the City of Albany, in the County of Albany. . . . (New York 1789). Broadside, fol.

By Alexander Hamilton.

Hamilton Papers V pp. 255-261; Mitchell pp. 38, 778; E. 21871. Query if E. 22185 is the same.

89-22 To the unbiassed & independent electors of the State of New York . . . April 7, 1789. Broadside.

By Jonathan Lawrence.

Hamilton Papers V p. 315. STE 45619; E. Supp. B7092 not attr.

89-23   A voyage around the world . . . Northwest coast of America . . .
        By Captain George Dixon. London . . . 1789. 4to. xxixp.,
        11., 360, 47p., 5fold. charts, 17pl., tab.; also 2d ed.

        By William Beresford.

        CHA 17926 3:4. S. 20364 not attributed.

89-24   The writings of Laco, as published in the Massachusetts Centinel
        . . . Boston, 1789. 8vo. 39p.

        By Stephen Higginson.

        E. 21886; S. 31748; Howes H. 468; DAB 9: 16.

1790

90-01   Address to the inhabitants of Alexandria, and other seaports
        . . . from a proprietor of lands on the Sioto. . . . 1790. 16mo.
        15p.

        By William Duer (?).

        Vail 804: "probably written by or for Colonel William Duer
        of New York City". S. 746; E. 22298 not attr.

90-02   Address to the people of Pennsylvania . . . proceedings against
        John Nicholson, comptroller-general. . . . Phila. . . . 1790 . . .
        8vo. 56p.

        By John Nicholson.

        E. 22735; S. 55226; D.A.B. 13:504.

90-03   Apperçu hazardé sur l'exportation dans les colonies. . . . Paris
        . . . 1790. 8vo. 64p.

        By Charles Hector, Count d'Estaing.

        S. 23031.

90-04   An authentic statement of all the facts relative to Nootka

Sound. . . . London . . . 1790. 8vo. (2)26p. Signed "Argonaut".

By John C. Etches.

S. 23087; Howes E206; CHA 6790 3: 2.

90-05   Congress. The residence law . . . late visit of our illustrious
President . . . An Inhabitant. . . . [Hagerstown? 1790] .
Broadside.

By Otho H. Williams.

E. Supp. B 7623; STE 46102.

90-06   A continuation of an authentic statement . . . Nootka Sound.
. . . London . . . 1790. 8vo. 1p.l., 34p. Signed "Argonaut".

By John C. Etches.

CHA 6790 3: 3; S. 23088; Howes E207. See no. 90-04.

90-07   The Contrast, a comedy. . . . Phila. . . . 1790. 8vo. xxiv, 79,
(1)p., front.

By Royall Tyler.

E. 22948; Hill 309; S. 97617; D.A.B. 19:96.

90-08   Doubts on the abolition of the slave trade; by an old member
of parliament. London . . . 1790. 8vo. 123p.

By John Ranby.

S. 20675, 67743+.

90-09   An essay on the culture of silk . . . by a citizen of Philadelphia.
. . . Philadelphia 1790. 8p.

By Pelatiah Webster?

Kress B. 2009 (supposed author). S. 102410 with "?". E.
22491 not attributed.

90-10   An essay on the African slave trade. Philadelphia . . . 1790. 8vo.
15p.

By William Belsham.

E. 22337. S. 22951 not attributed. S. 25499 attr. to Benjamin Franklin. Reprint from "Essays philosophical, historical, and literary" London 1789, p.(2), attributed to Belsham: Edinburgh p. 309; Lowndes Bibliographer's Manual of English Literature, London 1869, p. 152.

90-11   An historical journal of the expeditions, by sea and land, to the North of California . . . San Diego and Monte-Rey. . . . London . . . 1790: 1p., l., ii, 76p., 5fold. maps.

By Miguel Costanso.

CHA 18623 3: 7; S. 17020

90-12   The history of America, in two books. . . . Philadelphia . . . 1790. 12mo., viii, 260p., 2l., 2maps.

By Jedidiah Morse.

CHA 14935 2: 4; E. 22682 (in two states: printed on fine and on common paper); S. 50937.

90-13   Information to Europeans who are disposed to migrate to the United States . . . A citizen of Pennsylvania. . . . Philadelphia . . . (1790). 16mo. 16p.

By Benjamin Rush.

Reprinted in Rush, Essays (1798) E. 34495. See Butterfield, L. H., Letters of Benjamin Rush, Vol. 1, p. 549. Attr. to Mathew Carey E. 22390; Vail 806. S. 34702 not attributed.

90-14   In the Supreme Court of the United States. To . . . John Jay . . . sitting in chancery. . . . Phila. . . . (179- .) 28p. 35cm.

By William Lewis.

STE 45777.

90-15   Letters lately published . . . dispute with Spain . . . Verus. . . . London . . . 1790. 8vo. viii, 101p.

By James Bland Burges?

S. 40603.

90-16   Memoirs of the late Dr. Benjamin Franklin . . . his pamphlet . . .

"Information to those who would wish to remove to America".... London ... 1790. 8vo. 94p., front.

By   Wilmer.

CHA 7544 3:7. S. 25615 not attributed.

90-17   The memorial ... of the public creditors ... of Pennsylvania ... to ... Congress.... Philadelphia ... 1790. 8vo. 28p.

By Alexander James Dallas.

E. 22983. S. 47621 not attributed.

90-18   National credit and character.... Phila... 1790. 8vo. 4p. Caption title. Signed: B.

By John Beale Bordley.

E. Supp. B 7324; STE 45834.

90-19   Le nouveau Mississippi ... dangers ... du Scioto.... Paris ... 1790. 16mo. 44p. Also 8vo. (6)44p.

By Sergeant-Major Roux.

S. 73511; Howes R472; Vail 838; CHA 11360 3:3. S. 35512 attr. to Fr. Jacquemart.

90-20   A plan for a school ... Pennsylvania and New Jersey.... Philadelphia ... 1790. 8vo. 52p.

By Owen Biddle.

STE 22361.

90-21   A plan for the general arrangement of the militia of the United States.... New York 1790. Fol. 26p.

By Henry Knox.

E. 22988; Howes K220; S. 38161. First published 1786.

90-22   A plea for the poor soldiers ... must be paid. By a citizen of Philadelphia.... 1790. 8vo. iv(1)6-39p; also New Haven 33p.

By Pelatiah Webster.

E. 23060, 61; S. 102412; Jeff. 3153; Howes W210.

90-23   Réponse au champion Americain, ou colon très-aisé à connaitre
(Paris 1790). 8vo. 8p.

By M. Degouge(s?)

S. 19300.

90-24   A second address to the freemen . . . Connecticut. By Horatio
Juvenal. . . . (Litchfield 1790). 10p.

By Richard Alsop.

STE 22599. See no. 90-28.

90-25   The slave trade indispensible . . . by a West India merchant. . . .
London 1790. 8vo. (2)77(1)p.

By William Innes.

S. 82068.

90-26   Strictures on Mercer's introductory discourse . . . British debts.
London 1790. 8vo. 44(1)p.

By David Ross.

S. 92841. See E. 24538 and note. In answer to E. 21958.

90-27   A supplement to the essay on monies, coins, & c. . . . Philadelphia
. . . 1790. 8vo. (2)7p.

By John Beale Bordley.

E. 22368; S. 93803; Boyd 16:603; Kress S. 5213. See no.
89-12.

90-28   To the freemen . . . Connecticut . . . By Horatio Juvenal. . . .
(Hartford 1790). 10p.

By Richard Alsop.

STE. 22598.

90-29   A true and authentic history of his Excellency George Washington. . . . Philadelphia . . . 1790. 12mo., 23(1)p.

By Jedidiah Morse.

CHA 8492 2: 7. E. 22933, not seen, attributed to Thomas Thornton. S. 97086 that this extracts from Morse, with an ode by Thornton added.

90-30   Washington en Necker. Lierzang (Amsterdam) 1790. 8vo. (4)8p. Also London?

By Rhijnvis Feith?

S. 101893.

1791

91-01   An account of the soil, growing timber, and other productions . . . back parts of the State of New York and Pennsylvania. . . . Genesee . . . (London) 1791. Sm. fol. (3)2-37, (1)2-4, 39-45p. 2 maps.

By William Temple Franklin (?).

Vail 867: "probably" by Franklin. S. 26926; STE 23101; CHA 7913 2:5 not attr.

91-02   An address to the inhabitants of the District of Maine . . . separation . . . Massachusetts. By one of their fellow citizens. . . . Portland . . . 1791. 4to. 54p.

By Daniel Davis.

E. 23313; Vail 865; Noyes 29; Howes D107. Not attributed in S. 43903.

91-03   An address to the legislature . . . Connecticut . . . dividing the State into districts . . . By a citizen of Connecticut. New Haven . . . 1791. 8vo. 37p.

By William Pitt Beers.

E. 23165; Dex. 4p. 746; Trumb. 37.

91-04   An address to the people of Great Britain, on the propriety of
         abstaining from West India sugar and rum. London 1791.
         12p.; Birmingham 8p.; Glasgow 12p.

         By William Fox.

         S. 25378, 102813+; Kress B. 2078-80.

91-05   An address to the stock-holders of the Bank of North America
         . . . By a citizen of Philadelphia. . . . Philadelphia . . . 1791.
         8vo. 8p.

         By Pelatiah Webster?

         E. 23970; STE 23970: "apparently a ghost of 23971".
         See no. 91-20.

91-06   Authentic memoirs of William Augustus Bowles, Ambassador
         from . . . Creeks and Cherokees to the Court of London. . . .
         London . . . 1791. 12 mo; 2p.l. vi, 79p.

         By Captain (?) Bryan?

         Abernethy 98n. S. 7082 not attributed. CHA 2587 1:4,
         "by Benjamin Baynton, captain of a Penna. loyalist regi-
         ment."

91-07   A brief examination of Lord Sheffield's observations . . . com-
         merce of the United States . . . Philadelphia . . . 1791. 8vo.
         vii(1) 135(1)p.; also 39p.; also 48p.

         By Tench Coxe.

         E. 23295; S. 17294; B. Ath. p. 560; Howes C828; Kress
         B. 2066 (39p.); STE 23294 (48p.)

91-08   An extract from the proceedings of the South Carolina Yazoo
         Company. . . . Charleston . . . 1791 (10), 44, (2), 11, (2), 27,
         13(1)p. 4to.

         By Robert Goodloe Harper.

         E. 23783; Abernethy 76n.

91-09   Lessons to a young prince, by an old statesman, on the present
         disposition in Europe to a general revolution. . . . New York

... 1791. 8vo., (5)6-56, 49-68p., 5 plates. Also London,
2p., l., ivp., l., 182, 2p., 5 plates.

By David Williams.

CHA 25850 2: 6; 3: 1; STE 24001. E. 24002 is Philadelphia edition, not seen. S. 104186.

91-10   Letters addressed to the yeomanry ... injustice of ... indirect
taxation ... By a Farmer. Philadelphia ... 1791. 8vo. 47p.

By George Logan.

E. 23507; S. 39243 (Laughan); S. 41790 note; Tolles p. 111;
Jeff. 3156; Ford 47.

91-11   Observations on the evidence ... abolishing the slave trade. ...
London 1791. 8vo. 310p.

By John Ranby.

S. 67744.

91-12   Observations on the impolicy of recommencing the importation
of slaves ... by a citizen of South-Calolina [sic] (Charleston
1791) 11p.

By David Ramsay?

E. Supp. B7804 (Ramsay named on NcD copy)

91-13   The oracle of liberty, and mode ... free government. Philadelphia
... 1791. Signed "Hermes". 8vo. 39p.

By Caesar A. Rodney.

E. 23742; S. 72493; CHA 16489 2: 5; Howes R396. S.
31500 not attr.

91-14   The political crisis; or, a dissertation on the Rights of Man. ...
London ... 1791.

By Amos Stoddard?

D.A.B. 18:51. Not found in S. or Halk.

91-15   A short account ... slave trade and an address ... West India sugar and rum. Sevenoaks 1791. 8vo. 16p.

By William Fox?

The address is attributed to Fox (see no. 91-04). Not attr. S. 80582; Kress B. 2199.

91-16   A sketch of the life and projects of John Law of Lauriston. Comptroller general of the finances in France. . . . London, 1791. Fol., ii, 48p.; Also Edinburgh, 1791.

By John Philip Wood.

CHA 19904 3: 3; S. 105051; Edinburgh 3: 1271.

91-17   A topographical analysis of the Commonwealth of Virginia. . . . Richmond (1791). Broadside, fol. Also Philadelphia, same.

By William Tatham.

E. 23820,21; S. 94413,14; Davis 198.

91-18   To the free electors of the County of Suffolk . . . the office of the register of deeds. . . . Boston . . . 1791. Broadside.

By Samuel Ruggles.

STE 46276; E. Supp. B7815.

91-19   To the public. Some remarks on the proceedings of the late convention . . . By the author. . . . New Hampshire . . . 1791. 8vo., 31(1)p.

By Thomas Cogswell.

Turner, p. 49. Not attributed, E. 23834; S. 86747. Streeter 722 suggests Abel Foster (of Canterbury, N.H., should be Abiel).

91-20   To the stock-holders of the Bank of North-America, on the subject of the old and new banks (caption). . . . Philadelphia . . . 1791. Subscribed "A citizen of Philadelphia". 8vo. 16p.

By Pelatiah Webster.

STE 23971; S. 102416. See no. 91-05.

91-21   The triumph of truth . . . By John Paul Martin. . . . Boston . . .
1791. 8vo. 62p.

> By Abraham Bishop.

> E. 23207; S. 97010+; Dex. 4 p. 20. S. 44890 attr. to Mar-
tin.

1792

92-01   An abridgement of the evidence delivered before a select committee . . . abolition of the slave trade. London . . . 1792.
12mo. 24p.

> By William Fox.

> S. 93600+. See no. 92-34.

92-02   Address to the citizens of Ann Arundel and Prince George's
Counties. Annapolis . . . 1792. 12mo.

> By David Ross?

> STE 24756. (Origin of entry unknown)

92-03   An address to the people of Great Britain, on the propriety of
abstaining from West India sugar & rum. . . . New York . . .
1792. 12mo., 12p.; Also Boston . . . 1792. 8vo., 12p.;
Philadelphia . . .1792. 8vo., 12p., also 16(3)p.; Lancaster
. . . 1792. 8vo., 12p.

> By William Fox.

> S. 25378, 102813+; STE 46446,47; Kress B. 2296,97;
E. Supp. 7997,8; E. 24231, 24232. See no. 91-04. Includes no. 92-30, by Crafton.

92-04   An address to the public. (Baltimore, 1792). 16mo. 94p.

> By William Matthews.

> E. 24533; S. 46894; B. Ath. p. 140; Minick 80.

92-05   An appeal to the candour . . . people of England . . . West

India merchants. . . . London . . . 1792. xvi, 118p. Two editions, one with four lines of text p. xvi.

By   Macarty (Captain?)

Kress B. 2367; Kress S. 5379; Sabin 102788+. S. 1779 not attr.

92-06   A brief examination of Lord Sheffield's observations . . . commerce of the United States. . . . London . . . 1792. (8) (4) 135p.

By Tench Coxe.

Kress B. 2277; S. 17294; ((8)127p.). See no. 91-07.

92-07   The calumnies of Verus; or, Catholics vindicated from certain old slanders. . . . Philadelphia . . . 1792. 58p.

By Francis A. Fleming.

STE 24321; Finotti p. 116.

92-08   The case of the sugar colonies. London 1792. 97p.

By John Collins.

Kress B. 2265; S. 14441.

92-09   Colony commerce . . . United States. . . . London (1792). Subscribed Alexander Campbell Brown. 8vo. 88p.

By Mark Leavenworth.

Jeff. 3158; Dex. 3: 421. S. 8439 under Brown.

92-10   A description of Kentucky in North America . . . observations . . . United States. . . . (London) . . . 1792. 8vo., map., ivp. 2l.(1)6-121(1)p.

By Harry Toulmin.

E. 26268; S. 96327; Rich 1: 11; Vail 923; Howes T307; D.A.B. 18:601; CHA 6035 3:5. CHA notes this is the latter portion of no. 92-35. See "The Western Country in 1793", Marion Tinling and Godfrey Davies, eds., 1948, San Marino, Calif., pp. xv, xvi. E. has "(Lexington)". Reprinted 1945 CHA 6035 3: 7.

92-11   Description topographique de six cents mille acres de terres . . .
         (n. p.) 1792. 4to. 14,8p.

         By Pierre Chassanis?

         S. 19728, 95825+; Vail 899.

92-12   The duty of abstaining from the use of West India produce . . .
         London (1792). 23p.

         By William Allen.

         Kress B. 2243. S. 21473 not attr.

92-13   An enquiry into the constitutional authority of the supreme
         federal court . . . by a citizen of South-Carolina. . . .
         Charleston . . . 1792. Signed, Hortensius. 8vo. 49p.

         By Timothy Ford.

         E. 24324; Turnbull p. 290; S. 88111+; 93501+; Howes
         F256 (with question mark). Attributed to David Ramsey in
         S. 67684+. Not attributed in S. 22639.

92-14   An essay on the abolition, not only of the African slave trade,
         but of slavery in the British West Indies. London . . . 1792.
         8vo., 49p.

         By John Gray, LLD.

         Kress B. 2324; CHA 6769 2: 4. S. 22950, not attributed.

92-15   Five letters, addressed to the yeomanry . . . dangerous scheme
         of . . . secretary Hamilton to establish national manufac-
         tories . . . By a Farmer. Philadelphia . . . 1792. 8vo. 28p.

         By George Logan.

         E. 24480; Jeff. 3157; Ford 50; Tolles pp. 117, 118. S.
         39242 attr. to Dr. Laughan.

92-16   The foresters, An American tale; being a sequel to the history
         of John Bull the clothier. . . . Boston . . . 1792. 12mo., 216p.
         front.

         By Jeremy Belknap.

E. 24086; CHA 2039 3: 5, 6; S. 4433. The foresters represent the various states.

92-17   The history of Jack Nips. Albany . . . 1792. 8vo. 8p.

By John Leland.

E. 24469.

92-18   Letter to the members of Parliament . . . slave trade . . . by a West India merchant. London 1792. 8vo. (2)84p.

By William Innes.

S. 34788. S. 82004 not attr.

92-19   Minutes of Debates in Council, on the banks of the Ottawa River . . . Indian Nations, who defeated the Army of the United States. . . . Philadelphia . . . 1792. 8vo. (2), 22p.

By Alexander McKee?

See "The Month at Goodspeed's", Vol. 34 at p. 215. Not attributed in E. 24647, 25653. See no. 00-34.

92-20   Observations on Paine's Rights of Man . . . by Publicola. . . . Edinburgh . . . (1792). 8vo. 48p.

By John Quincy Adams.

Cronin & Wise, J. Q. Adams 146; Malone Vol. 2, p. 363-6; Brant, 1787-1800, p. 340. Has 8 of 11 letters from Columbian Centinel.

92-21   The path to riches . . . some thoughts respecting a bank for the Commonwealth. By a citizen of Massachusetts. . . . Boston . . . 1792. 8vo. 77p.

By James Sullivan.

E. 24829; S. 93504; D.A.B. 18:191; Hamilton Papers xi p. 501, 2. "A sharp attack on Hamilton's banking policies": Dauer p. 69.

92-22   The Politicks and views of a certain party, displayed. Printed in the year 1792. 8vo. 36p.

By William Loughton Smith (very likely with the close col-
laboration of Alexander Hamilton).

E. 24801; S. 84830; Ford 49; B. Ath. p. 188; Howes S.
712; DAB 17: 365; Hamilton Papers xiii p. 393. (See
Brant, 1787-1800, p. 365.) Attr. to Alexander Hamilton in
S. 29973.

92-23   Public good: being an examination into the claim of Virginia
to the vacant western territory . . . By the author of Common sense. . . . Albany . . . (1792) 8vo., 41p.

By Thomas Paine.

CHA 16736 3:1; E. 24658 includes this; Howes P. 30. E.
16920 is 1780 edition.

92-24   Reflections offertes aux capitalistes de L'Europe, sur les béné-
fices . . . dans les États-Unis. . . . Amsterdam . . . 1792. 8vo.
1p., l., 3p., 6-42p., map, tab.

By Captain Benjamin Van Pradelles.

Vail 926; S. 98538; Howes V39; CHA 7916 3: 2.

92-25   Reflexions on the state of the Union. . . . Philadelphia . . . 1792.
8vo. 38p.

By Tench Coxe.

E. 24230; S. 17302; Jeff. 3629.

92-26   The rights of suffrage . . . Hudson. . . . 1792. Signed, "Plain
sense". 12mo. 45(1)p.

By Joshua Sands?

E. 24769. STE 24769; S. 71378 not attr.

92-27   A second address to the people of Great Britain . . . West India
sugar. . . . Rochester 1792. 8vo. 11p.

By Major-General A. Burn?

S. 102865.

92-28   The security of the rights of citizens in . . . Connecticut considered. . . . Hartford . . . 1792. 8vo. 102(2)p.

By Zephaniah Swift?

Not attr. in E. 24776, S. 15854 or Trumb. 1345. Not Dex.
Compiler has copy noted in contemporary hand: "By Zeph^h
Swift". Copy also notes: "W. Williams bot of H & G sigd
(signed?) p. 1/6". The Library of the late James Hammond
Trumbull, American Art Association, 1921, has "Swift (J.)".

92-29 A short address to the people of Scotland, on the subject of the
slave trade. . . . Edinburgh . . . 1792. 8vo., 30p., 1l.

By   Houldbrooke.

CHA 9527 1: 2; S. 80593; Edinburgh 2: 433; Kress B.
2344.

92-30 A short sketch of the evidence for the abolition of the slave
trade . . . House of Commons. . . . Philadelphia . . . 1792.
12mo., 28, 16, (3)p.

By William Bell Crafton.

E. 24233. Included in E. 24292 over the initials W. B. C.
Included in no. 92-03.

92-31 Sketches on rotations of crops. . . . Philadelphia . . . 1792. 8vo.
(2)47p.; also with "alterations" slip; also Talboton (Md.)
1792 (2)47p., errata slip, ("on the rotation").

By John Beale Bordley.

E. 24129; STE 46390; E. Supp. B 7935. Compiler has Phila.
ed. with "alterations" slip bound in after final leaf of text.

92-32 Slavery inconsistent with justice and good policy. By Philanthropos. Lexington . . . 1792. 12mo. 34p.

By David Rice.

E. 24741; 5 A.I.I. 18; Howes R246; Jillson p. 13; Jeff.
1675; D.A.B. 15:537.

92-33 Strictures and observations upon the three executive depart-
ments. . . . By Massachusettensis. . . . 1792. 8vo. 32p.

By Daniel Leonard?

Howes L259; Wise & Cronin 557; Beard 230n; CHA 12530
2:3 "supposed author". Not attr. by E. 24515; or S. 92828; or
Ford 51. Attr. to Leonard in S. 40101. Ford says this an error.

92-34   A summary of the evidence produced before a Committee of
          the House of Commons, relating to the slave trade. . . . Lon-
          don . . . 1792. 16p.; 4 ed., 16mo., 8p; 6 ed. 8vo. 8p.

          By William Fox.

          CHA 20950 3: 1; S. 25380, 93600; Kress B. 2298 (16p.).
          See no. 92-01.

92-35   Thoughts on emigration . . . account of the State of Kentucky.
          London 1792. 8vo. vi(1)8-24, iv(1)6-121(3)p. map.

          By Harry Toulmin.

          S. 96328; Vail 924; Howes T308; Clark vol. 2, p. 156;
          Kress B. 2429. See no. 92-10.

92-36   To The Printer of the Maryland herald. . . . (Easton?) 1792.
          Signed "Republican". 8vo. 24p.

          By Joseph Hopper Nicholson.

          Minick 85; STE. 29646.

1793

93-01   An account of the rise, progress and termination of the
          malignant fever. . . . Phila. . . . 1793. 8vo., 36, 12p.

          By James Hardie?

          Austin, 15, suggests. E. 25075 not attributed.

93-02   The American Revolution: written in the style of ancient
          history . . . Vol. 1. Philadelphia . . . 1793. 12mo. xii,
          226p.

By Richard Snowden.

E. 26179; CHA 20152 2:1. See no. 94-03.

93-03   An answer to Pain's (sic) Rights of Man. By John Adams, Esq.
         . . . London . . . 1793. 8vo. 48p; also 12mo. 34p.; also
         Dublin 8vo. 48p. (seven letters).

By John Quincy Adams.

See no. 92-20, which has one more letter. Bartlett 3574 (34p.)

93-04   Biographical sketch of the life & character of his late excellency
         Governor Hancock. Boston (1793) 16mo., 16p.; also 12mo.,
         11p.

By James Sullivan.

E. 26234, 26235; S. 93493+, 93494. S. 30180 not attributed.

93-05   Candid animadversions on a petition . . . General Assembly of
         Maryland . . . flagrant injustice . . . in favour of a particular
         denomination of christians. By Vindex. Baltimore . . . 1793.
         8vo. (5)47p.

By Patrick Allison.

S. 99771; STE 25444; Minick 100.

93-06   A Case decided in the Supreme Court of the United States . . .
         Whether a State be liable to be sued by a private citizen. . . .
         Philadelphia . . . 1793. 8vo. (2)120(1)p. (two issues); also
         Boston 8vo. 80p.

By Alexander James Dallas.

E. 25370, 71; B. Ath. p. 64. S. 11308 not attr.

93-07   The Declaration of Independence: a poem . . . By a citizen of
         Boston. . . . Boston 1793. 8vo. 24p.

By George H. Richards.

E. 26084; S. 70917; CHA 9826 3: 1; Weg. 329.

93-08   Description . . . du territoire . . . au sud de l'Ohio. . . . (Paris

1793?) 8vo., 28p.

By Daniel Smith.

Howes S. 587.

93-09   A description of the situation . . . land in the District of Maine.
        . . . (Phila. 1793). 4to. 44p.

        By Benjamin Lincoln. (Also attributed to William Bingham.)

        E. 25720; Sibley XII: 438. Howes M226 "probably". See
        note to S. 5459. D.A.B. 2:278 ascribes to Bingham.

93-10   An examination of the late proceedings in Congress, respecting
        the official conduct of the Secretary of the Treasury . . .
        Printed within the United States. 1793. 8vo. 28p. Editions
        dated on p. 3, 8th March 1793 and 20th October 1793, re-
        spectively.

        By James Monroe, assisted by James Beckley.

        Attribution from: " 'The Piece Left Behind': Monroe's
        authorship . . . revealed" by Edmund and Dorothy Smith
        Berkeley. Va. Mag. of Hist. and Biog., April 1967. Attributed
        to John Taylor CHA 6900 2: 3; E. 26245; S. 94490; Ford
        53; B. Ath. p. 197; Mitchell p. 267; Malone 3: p. 28 and
        note. S. 29952 not attr.

93-11   Excise, the favorite system of aristocrats . . . taxes are drawn
        from the laborious part of the community. . . . (Philadelphia
        1793). Broadside 42x26 cm.

        By George Logan.

        Tolles p. 131; E. Supp. B8399; STE 48115 (1797).

93-12   The federal or new ready reckoner and traders useful assistant
        . . . the first edition. Chesnuthill . . . 1793. 8vo. (2) (2)
        (120) 5 tables (4)p.

        By Daniel Fenning.

        E. 25475. S. 23977 not attr. Published at the same time in
        German E. 25476.

93-13   Historia de la ultima guerra . . . los Estados-Unidos . . . Alcala.
         1793. 4to. 2vols.

         By Jonathan Boucher.

         S. 6841.

93-14   The history of Jack Nips. . . . Concord . . . 1793; Dover . . .
         1793. 12mo. 23p.; Windsor . . . 1793. 12mo. 12p.;
         Printed in Massachusetts 1793. 16p. 19cm.

         By John Leland.

         E. 25714-6; STE 46807; E. Supp. B8395. See no. 92-17.

93-15   Les Français libres à leurs frères les Canadiens. (Philadelphia
         1793). 12mo. 8p. (caption title)

         By Edmond Charles Genet.

         Jeff. 3243; E. Supp. B8346; STE 46758.

93-16   A letter, commercial and political . . . the real interests of
         Britain . . . by Jasper Wilson. London . . . 1793. 8vo.
         (4)3-86p.; also second ed. 8vo. (4)72p.; Also third ed.,
         same; also Dublin 8vo. 70p.

         By Dr. James Currie.

         Hamilton Papers xv pp. 152-4; S. 104646; Kress
         B. 2473-5.

93-17   Letters addressed to the yeomanry of the United States, con-
         taining some observations on funding and bank systems:
         by an American Farmer. . . . Philadelphia: 1793. 8vo. 24p.

         By George Logan.

         E. 25724; Ford 52; Kress B. 2570; Tolles p. 125.

93-18   Letters from an American farmer . . . by J. Hector St. John.
         . . . Philadelphia . . . 1793. 12mo. 240p.

         By M. G. St. Jean de Crevecoeur.

         E. 25357. First published London 1782.

93-19   Liberte Egalite. Les Francais Libres à leurs frères de la
        Louisiane. (Phila. 1793). 12mo. 8p. (caption).

        By Edmond Charles Genet.

        Jeff. 3244; E. Supp. B. 8347; STE 46759.

93-20   A military essay . . . South Carolina. . . . Charleston . . . 1793.
        8vo. 12p.

        By James Simmons (or Simons).

        E. 26163. See E. 32838 as to name.

93-21   Observations on conventions, made in a Tammanial debate.
        Published at the request of the Society. New-York . . .
        1793. 12mo. 13p.

        By William Pitt Smith.

        E. 26176; S. 84843.

93-22   Observations on the present war . . . emancipation of the
        slaves . . . Sunderland. . . . (1793). 8vo. (2)61p.

        By John Hampson.

        S. 30148.

93-23   Observations on the River Potomack . . . and the City of Wash-
        ington. New-York . . . 1793. 8vo. 29p., plan.

        By Tobias Lear.

        E. 25711; Jeff. 4043; S. 101944; Howes L166 (also attr.
        to Andrew Ellicott); B. Ath. p. 121; Clark, Ed. 2: 102.
        Jeff. has 32 leaves. D.A.B. 9:76.

93-24   Observations upon the revolution in France. . . . Boston . . .
        1793. 8vo. (4)44p.

        By Charles Crawford.

        E. 25356.

93-25   Old truths and established facts . . . by Vindex. (London 1793)
        8vo. 13p.

By Thomas Paine?

S. 57147, 99776+. In answer to S. 99320. Kress S. 5406 has 1792.

93-26 The Patriot . . . affairs in Britain and in France. With observations on Republican Government, and . . . Thomas Paine. . . . Edinburgh . . . 1793. 8vo. (4)76p.

By Thomas Hardy, D.D.

Edinburgh 2: 252. S. 59081 not attributed. "America . . . cannot go on long . . . their union at this moment depends on the life of a single man, the president . . ." p. 52.

93-27 A Plan for encouraging agriculture and increasing the value of farms . . . Pennsylvania. . . . (Phila. 1793). 12mo. 11p.

By Tench Coxe.

E. 25355. S. 63266 not attr., suggests "about 1790".

93-28 A plea for literature: more especially the literature of free states. By a member of the old Congress. . . . Charleston . . . 1793. 12mo. (2)(2)119p.

By Richard Beresford.

E. 25162. Not attributed in S. 63384. See E. 26642 for advertisement naming the author.

93-29 Remarks on the American Universal Geography. By J. F. Boston . . . 1793. 8vo. 61(1)p.

By James Freeman.

CHA 7578 1: 6; E. 25510; S. 25764; Bartlett 3610.

93-30 A short description of the Tennassee [sic] government . . . south of the river Ohio. . . . Philadelphia . . . 1793. 8vo. 20p. Map sometimes added.

By Daniel Smith.

E. 26168; Howes S587 (26p.); S. 82420; Vail 955: D.A.B. 17: 254. See no. 96-72.

93-31 Some farraginous remarks upon an act . . . Lord's day. By a lover of the truth. Concord 1793. 22(1)p.

By Joseph Haynes.

STE 25593; S. 86643.

93-32 To the inhabitants of the United States west of the Alleghany. . . . (Lexington 1793). Broadside 39.5x31.5cm.

By John Breckinridge?

See Harrison p. 55. Not attributed E. Supp. B. 8319; STE 46730.

93-33 To the President and Congress . . . the remonstrance of the citizens west of the Allegany Mountains. . . . (Lexington 1793). Broadside 55.5x22cm.

By John Breckinridge.

Harrison p. 55. Not attributed E. Supp. B. 8320; STE 46731.

1794

94-01 An Address to the people of South-Carolina, by the general committee. . . . Charleston . . . 1794. Signed "Appius". 8vo. (2), i-vi, (1)4-42p.

By Robert Goodloe Harper.

E. 27092; S. 87733; Turnbull 299.

94-02 The Age of infidelity: in answer to Thomas Paine's Age of Reason. By a Layman . . . Boston . . . 1794. 12mo. 47p.; New York 52p., 59p., 59(1)p.; Philadelphia 70p.; Worcester 60p.

By Thomas Williams.

E. 28096,97, 28099, 28100; STE 47329,30; E. Supp. B. 9001,2.

94-03 The American Revolution; written in the style of ancient history. . . . Philadelphia . . . 1794. Vol. 2, 12mo., (2), (9)216p.

By Richard Snowden.

CHA 20152 2: 1; E. 27716. See No. 93-02 for Vol. 1.

94-04   Circulaire addressé . . . à tous les Habitans de la Louisiane. (New Orleans 1794). 4to. 5p.

By Baron de Carondelet.

E. 28983; Mitchell 637 n. 30.

94-05   City of Washington. The Advantageous situation. . . . Subscribers . . . form . . . a Society for . . . investing a Capital. . . . (Phila. 1794). Fol. broadside; also 4to. (2)p. Signed "J. G."

By James Greenleaf.

S. 101929; E. 27068 broadside.

94-06   The Constitutionalist . . . enquiry . . . Constitution of South-Carolina. . . . By Americanus. Charleston . . . 1794. 8vo. 55p.

By Timothy Ford.

E. 26987; S. 87811; Howes F255; Turnbull p. 303; Beard p. 221. Reply to no. 94-01.

94-07   The contrast . . . speech of King George III . . . and the speech of President George Washington. . . . London, 1794. 8vo. 24p.

By John Williamson.

S. 104459; S. 16180 not attr.; Halk 1-427.

94-08   A Definition of parties; or the political effects of the paper system considered. Philadelphia, April 5th, 1794. . . . Philadelphia . . . 1794. 8vo. 16p.

By John Taylor.

STE. 26861; E. 27781; S. 94489; D.A.B. 18:332; Simms 216; Beard 196n; Davis 403. Not attributed in E. 26861; S. 19272.

94-09   Democracy: An epic poem, By Aquiline Nimble-Chops, Demo-
         crat. . . . New York . . . (1794). 8vo. 20p.

         By Henry Brockholst Livingston.

         E. 28979 (1794); S. 41608 ("about 1790"). "The Echo"
         (no. 07-07) p. 196 dates March 1794.

94-10   An Enquiry into the Principles and Tendency of certain Public
         Measures. Philadelphia . . . 1794. 8vo. (4)92p.

         By John Taylor.

         E. 27782; S. 94489+; Ford 56; Jeff. 3175; Howes T61;
         D.A.B. 18:332; Simms 216. Not attr. in S. 22647.

94-11   The examiners examined: being a defence of the Age of Rea-
         son. . . . New York . . . 1794. . . . 8vo. 84p. front.

         By Elihu Palmer.

         D.A.B. 14:178. E. 26954 not attributed.

94-12   Extract of a letter from a gentleman in America to a friend in
         England, on . . . Emigration. (London, 1794). 8vo. 11p.
         Also 8vo. 16p.

         By Thomas Cooper.

         S. 16611. See no. 94-34.

94-13   Germanicus. (Letters to the citizens of the United States.)
         (1794). 8vo. 77p., errata.

         By Edmund Jennings Randolph.

         E. 27597; S. 67812; Howes R53.

94-14   The history of Jack Nips. . . . Exeter . . . 1794. 12p.

         By John Leland.

         STE 47097; E. Supp. B. 8722. See no. 93-14.

94-15   Intimations; on manufactures . . . trade interfering . . . in
         foreign markets. (Signed B.) Philadelphia (1794). 8vo. 8p.

         By John Beale Bordley.

E. 26681. (See S. 6415.) Reprinted no. 96-73.

94-16   Letters on emigration. By a gentleman, lately returned from
         America. London . . . 1794. 8vo. (4)76p.

         By John (?) Hodgkinson.

         Cush. 1p. 113; Halk. 3p. 334; Vail 983; Kress S. 5452;
         Howes H559. Not attr. in S. 22502 or S. 40615.

94-17   Letters on the crimes of George III . . . by an American officer.
         . . . Paris (1794). 8vo. 80, 135p.; also in French, Paris
         (1794). 8vo. xi 80, 135p.

         By General John S. Eustace.

         S. 23117, 18; Howes E. 212.

94-18   The life of General Washington, commander in chief. . . .
         Philadelphia . . . 1794. 24mo., 36p., 2 ports.

         By Jedidiah Morse.

         CHA 14935 2: 7; S. 101841; Baker 13; STE 27221 (p. 543).

94-19   Manlius; with notes and references. (Boston 1794). 8vo. 56p.;
         also 54p.

         By Christopher Gore.

         E. 27062, 27063; S. 28016; Beard 237n; CHA 2:4,5.

94-20   Memorandums . . . respecting plunder taken after a siege. . . .
         London. 1794. 8vo. (4)106p.

         By Sir Henry Clinton.

         Howes C495.

94-21   A narrative of the proceedings of the black people, during . . .
         calamity in Philadelphia, in . . . 1793. . . . By A. J. and R. A.
         Phila. . . . 1794. 8vo. 28p.

         By Absalom Jones and Richard Allen.

         E. 27170; S. 36442; Austin 1079.

94-22   Noticias de la provincia de Californias . . . Valencia. 1794.

16mo. 104, 96, 104p. 2 fold. tab.

By Father Luis Sales.

S. 75765; Howes S52; Bartlett 3637 (18mo.). Not attributed S. 38381, 56007.

94-23   Observations on the emigration of Dr. Joseph Priestley, and on
. . . addresses delivered . . . at New-York. Philadelphia 1794
(no copy known); also New York 1794 (3)4-40p. (title has
"Priestly"); also London eds. 1794: Stockdale (3)4-63(1)p.
(two issues); Richarson (3)4-63(1)p.; Richarson (3)4-
30p., plus a variant.

By William Cobbett.

Gaines 2a-2g; E. 26777, 78; S. 13899.

94-24   Observations on the proposed bill . . . explain the law. . . .
Easton (Md.) 1794. Sm. 4to. 43p.

By John Leeds Bozman.

Minick 155. Not attributed in E. 27433 or S. 56554.

94-25   Observations on the River Potomack . . . and the City of
Washington. . . . New York . . . 1794. 12mo. 30p.,
front., plan.

By Tobias Lear.

E. 27209; S. 39533, 101944. See no. 93-23. S. 64584 is
Amsterdam edition (1794).

94-26   Outlines of a plan, for establishing a State Society of Agriculture. . . . Phila. . . 1794. 8vo. (2), (11)p.

By John Beale Bordley.

E. 26682.

94-27   The political progress of Britain . . . part first, second edition.
. . . Philadelphia 1794. 8vo. 80p.

By James Thomson Callender.

E. 26725; S. 10066, 63795+.

THE

POLITICIAN OUT-WITTED,

A

C O M E D Y,

IN FIVE ACTS.

Written in the YEAR 1788.

By an A M E R I C A N.

" Then let not Cenfure, with malignant joy,
" The harveft of his humble hope deftroy!"
Falconer's Shipwreck.

N E W - Y O R K:

PRINTED FOR THE AUTHOR, BY W. ROSS, IN BROAD-STREET,
AND SOLD BY THE DIFFERENT BOOKSELLERS.

M.DCC.LXXXIX.

Attributed to Samuel Low. No. 89-14.

A N

E S S A Y

ON THE

AFRICAN

SLAVE TRADE.

———

PHILADELPHIA:

Printed by DANIEL HUMPHREYS, in Front-
street, near the Drawbridge.

M. DCC. XC.

Attributed to William Belsham. No. 90-10.

OBSERVATIONS

ON

PAINE's RIGHTS OF MAN,

IN A

SERIES OF LETTERS,

BY *PUBLICOLA.*

It is not a mechanical horror againſt the name of a King, or of ariſtocracy, nor a phyſical antipathy to the ſound of an extravagant title, or to the ſight of an innocent ribband, that can authoriſe a people to lay violent hands upon the Conſtitution.　　　　LETTER V.

EDINBURGH:

Printed and Sold by J. DICKSON, and all the Bookſellers of Scotland.

[*PRICE SIXPENCE.*]

AN

ENQUIRY

INTO THE

Principles and Tendency

OF CERTAIN

PUBLIC MEASURES.

PHILADELPHIA:

PRINTED BY THOMAS DOBSON, No. 41, SOUTH
SECOND-STREET.
M DCC XCIV.

Attributed to John Taylor. No. 94-10.

THE

ALTAR OF *BAAL*

THROWN DOWN:

OR, THE

FRENCH NATION

DEFENDED,

AGAINST THE

PULPIT SLANDER

OF

DAVID OSGOOD, A. M.

PASTOR of the CHURCH in *MEDFORD*.

A SERMON,

PAR CITOYEN DE NOVION.

OSGOOD ! " Stand forth, I dare thee to be tried,
" In that GREAT COURT where CONSCIENCE must preside."

BOSTON:
FROM THE Chronicle-Press, BY *ADAMS* & *LARKIN*.
M,DCC,XCV.

Attributed to James Sullivan. No. 95-02.

A

BONE to GNAW,

FOR THE

DEMOCRATS;

O R,

OBSERVATIONS

O N

A PAMPHLET,

ENTITLED,

" *The Political Progress of Britain.*"

PHILADELPHIA:

PRINTED for the PURCHASERS.

1795.

Attributed to William Cobbett. No. 95-05.

THE

GUILLOTINA,

OR A

DEMOCRATIC DIRGE,

A

POEM.

By the AUTHOR of the "DEMOCRATIAD."

" For here the deadly fecret's told,
" Who 'tis that fingers foreign gold;
" That " patriots" ftripp'd to ftate of nature,
" Bear ftrong refemblance to the traitor;
" That each diforganizing fcoffer,
" Will take a bribe if any offer.
" Come then ye ʼemocratic band,
" Who yearn to enthrall this favor'd land,
" To Edmund's difmal tomb draw near,
" And vent your lamentations here,
" In groans, as Rachel groan'd at Rama,
": *Hic cimis*—but—*ubique fama.*"

PHILADELPHIA:

SOLD AT
THE POLITICAL BOOK-STORE,
South Front-Street,
No. 8.

AN

EXAMINATION

OF THE

CONDUCT

OF THE

EXECUTIVE OF THE UNITED STATES,

TOWARDS THE

FRENCH REPUBLIC;

LIKEWISE

AN ANALYSIS OF THE EXPLANATORY ARTICLE OF THE BRITISH TREATY—IN A SERIES OF LETTERS.

BY A

CITIZEN OF PENNSYLVANIA.

"*There's something rotten in the State of Denmark!*"

Shakespeare.

PHILADELPHIA:

PRINTED BY FRANCIS AND ROBERT BAILEY, AT YORICK'S-HEAD, No. 116, HIGH-STREET.

M,DCC,XCVII.

Attributed to Albert Gallatin. No. 97-19.

94-28 The present state of learning in the College of New York. New
       York 1794. 8vo. 16p.

       By Samuel L. Mitchill.

       E. 27331; S. 49747.

94-29 Report of a case . . . Kamper . . . constitutionality . . . by a
       gentleman of the bar. Philadelphia . . . 1794. 8vo. 104p.

       By William Tatham.

       E. 27777; S. 94411.

94-30 Republican government advocated. A discourse delivered on
       the fourth of July, 1794. Elizabethtown . . . 1794. 8vo.
       16p.

       By Solomon Froeligh.

       E. 27024.

94-31 A review of the revenue system adopted by the first Congress
       . . . By a Citizen. Phila. 1794. 8vo. (4)130p.

       By William Findley.

       E. 26973; S. 70265; Howes F135; Mitchell 671n.65. Oliver
       Wolcott preferred Abraham Baldwin as author, quoted in E.
       S. 24363 is ii, 33p.

94-32 The Revolution in France, considered in respect to its progress
       and effects. By an American. . . . New York . . . 1794. 8vo.
       72p.

       By Noah Webster, Jr.

       E. 28053; S. 102395; Skeel 721; Morse 101.

94-33 A short account of Algiers . . . rupture between Algiers and the
       United States. . . . Philadelphia . . . 1794. 8vo., 1p., l., 46p.,
       front, fold. map; also second edition, same, 50p., l., front,
       fold. map.

       By Mathew Carey.

       E. 26732, 3; CHA 3844 1: 6, 7. S. 80578, 80579, not attr.

94-34   Thoughts on emigration, in a letter from a gentleman in Phila-
         delphia . . . London 1794. 8vo. (2)17p.

         By Thomas Cooper.

         S. 95677+. S. 22509 not attr. See no. 94-12.

94-35   Thoughts on the state of the American Indians. By a Citizen
         of the United States. New York . . . 1794. Signed,
         Lycurgus. 8vo. 36p.

         By Silas Wood.

         E. 28126; S. 105072; CHA 4516 2:2; Howes W641.

94-36   A view of the relative situation of Great Britain and the United
         States . . . By a merchant. London . . . 1794. 8vo. (4)43p.

         By Henry Merrtins Bird.

         S. 5542, 99578+; Cush. 1p192; Halk. 6p170; Howes B461.
         See Rogers 274 n. 112.

94-37   The Yankee spy. Calculated for the religious meridian of Mas-
         sachusetts . . . By Jack Nips. Boston . . . (1794). 12mo. 20p.

         By John Leland.

         E. 27215; S. 105973. S. 55350, under Nips, not attributed.
         STE 27215 is 20,4p.

1795

95-01   An address, from the Council of Proprietors of the Western
         division of New-Jersey . . . remarks . . . by Aristides. (Burling-
         ton) 1795. 12mo. 22p.

         By William Griffith.

         E. 28773; D.A.B. 7:625,6. DuPuy 2418 preferred Wm. P. Van
         Ness.

95-02   The Altar of Baal thrown down: or the French Nation defended

against the pulpit slander . . . Par Citoyen de Novion . . .
Boston 1795. 8vo. 31p. (two issues, one without half title
or tail piece). Also Philadelphia, 32p.; Stockbridge, 28p.

By James Sullivan.

E. 29585, 29587, 29588; S. 93492,93; Morse 129. S.
93492 questions any second Boston issue.

95-03   The American remembrancer . . . essays . . . Treaty with Great
         Britain. Phila. 1795. 3vols. 8vo. 288, 288, 312p.

         Mathew Carey, editor.

         E. 28389; Howes C138.

95-04   Aristocracy. An epic poem . . . Phila. . . . 1795. 8vo. 16p.
         Also book second, 17p.

         By Richard Alsop or David Humphreys.

         E. 28171,2, prefers Alsop. Not attr. in Weg. 494, 495.

95-05   A bone to gnaw, for the Democrats . . . Philadelphia . . . 1795.
         8vo. (3)iv,v(2)2-66p.; plus second edition (3)iv,v(2)41,
         3-66p. (two issues); plus third edition, same collation.

         By William Cobbett.

         Gaines 3a-3d; E. 28431-33; S. 13875; Pearl 5. For Part
         II see no. 95-36.

95-06   A brief exposition of the leading principles of a bank . . .
         Legislature of Maryland. Baltimore . . . 1795. 8vo. 45p.

         By James McHenry.

         E. 29010; B. Ath. p. 130; Minick 240. Not attr. in S.
         45091.

95-07   A candid examination of the objections to the treaty of
         amity . . . Great Britain . . . addressed to the citizens of S.
         Carolina. Charleston 1795. By a citizen of South Carolina.
         8vo. 42p. Also New York 2p.l.(1)4-43p., 1.5p.

         By William Loughton Smith.

E. 29534; S. 10663, 84819; Turnbull p. 320; Howes S710; B. Ath. p. 188; Rogers 279; Kress B3040 (New York). See no. 95-18.

95-08   Cautionary hints to Congress, respecting the sale of the western lands, belonging to the United States . . . Philadelphia . . . 1795. Signed, Columbus. 8vo. 15p.

By Col. James Wood?

S. 105034 suggests Wood; Vail 1013 not attr.; E. 28459 not attr.; E. 35760 suggests all Columbus entries were James Madison; E. 36457 changes attr. of E. 35760 (no. 99-27) to St. George Tucker.

95-09   The Columbiad: or, a poem on the American war, in thirteen cantoes. Philadelphia . . . 1795. Pref. signed "A New-Jersey Farmer". 8vo. (4)46p.

By Richard Snowden.

E. 29539; S. 85591; B. Ath. p. 190; CHA 4879 2:1.

95-10   Common Sense: or, natural ideas opposed to supernatural . . . New-York 1795. 8vo. 203(1)p.

By Constantin F. Chasseboeuf, Comte de Volney.

E. 29820; Morse 107n.

95-11   Decisions of cases in Virginia . . . with remarks . . . Richmond . . . 1795. fol. 165(1) (22)p.

By George Wythe.

E. 29930; S. 100230, 105703+. Copyright by Wythe.

95-12   A Defence of the treaty . . . Great Britain . . . under the signature of Camillus. New-York. 1795. 8vo. 139p.

By Alexander Hamilton.

E. 28795; S. 29951; Ford 58; CHA 3427 3:6; Kress B2967.

95-13   The Democratiad, a poem, in retaliation for the "Philadelphia

Jockey Club" . . . By a Gentleman of Connecticut. Philadelphia . . . 1795. 8vo. 22p. Also 2d ed. 8vo. 22(1)p.

By Lemuel Hopkins.

E. 28853, 28854; S. 95799; Weg. 206; Wandell p. 126;
D.A.B. 9:215.

95-14   The Democrat; or, intrigues and adventures of Jean Le Noir
. . . New York 1795. 2v. 16mo. (12)136; (4)162p.

By Henry James Pye.

E. 29375; S. 66861; Howes P665.

95-15   A description of Occacock inlet . . . directions to sail . . . Newbern 1795. (2)8p. map.

By Jonathan Price.

STE 29351; Wheat 582.

95-16   The Echo: or, a satirical poem on the virtuous ten . . . song on
the Treaty . . . Hartford 1795. 12mo. 22p.

By Lemuel Hopkins.

E. 28855; Weg. 204.

95-17   Examination of the treaty of amity . . . Great Britain, in several
numbers; by Cato. New-York . . . 1795. 8vo. 96p.

By Robert R. Livingston.

E. 28980; Howes L399; Ford 59; (S. 31747 attr. to Stephen
Higginson); D.A.B. 11:323; CHA 8847 3:1 (12 mo.). S.
29954 attr. to Alexander Hamilton.

95-18   The eyes opened, or the Carolinians convinced, by . . . representative in the Congress . . . Governor Jay's late treaty . . .
New-York . . . 1795. 8vo., l., 43p., l., 5p.

By William Loughton Smith.

E. 29535; S. 23545, 84819; Jeff. 3181; Turnbull p. 320;
CHA 3776 2:7. See no. 95-07 for earlier editions (B.Ath. p.
188 and Jeff. say it is later).

95-19   Features of Mr. Jay's Treaty . . . commerce of the United
        States . . . Philadelphia . . . 1795. 8vo. (2)51p.

        By Alexander James Dallas.

        E. 28527; Howes D26; B. Ath. p. 64; D.A.B. 5:38. (Attr.
        Mathew Carey in Rowe.) Not attr. in S. 23966. CHA 5725
        3:2 has 51p.

95-20   The Federal Ready Reckoner . . . Worcester 1795. 12mo.
        139(1)p.

        By Daniel Fenning.

        E. 28666. S. 23978 not attr. See no. 93-12.

95-21   An historical account . . . canal navigation in Pennsylvania . . .
        Phila. . . . 1795. 4to. (16), 77p., map; also (2), (16), 77p.,
        map; also (2), (16), 80p., map.

        By William Smith, provost, or Robert Morris.

        S. 50865; Kress B3003: Morris; S. 84620; STE 47605;
        E. Supp. B9298: Smith; E. 29474: Morris or Smith;
        NYPL 1155: Smith; Howes S692 favors Smith.

95-22   An historical journal of the American war . . . Boston 1795.
        8vo. (2)206p.

        By Thomas Pemberton.

        E. 29283.

95-23   The history of America in two books . . . The second edition
        . . . Philadelphia . . . 1795. 12mo., viii, 356p., 2fold. maps.

        By Jedidiah Morse.

        CHA 14935 2:6; E. 29111. See no. 90-12.

95-24   A Kick for a Bite . . . by Peter Porcupine . . . Philadelphia . . .
        1795. 8vo. (5)6-31(1)p.; plus a variant.

        By William Cobbett.

        Gaines 4a, b; E. 28436; S. 13886; Pearl 6. (The "Bite"
        was by Samuel Harrison Smith).

95-25   A letter from a gentleman to his friends in England . . . Canada
         . . . Philadelphia . . . 1795. 12mo. 30p. Also London 1795.

         By John Cosens Ogden?

         E. 29236. Questioned STE 29236. Not attr. S. 10504.

95-26   Letters of Franklin, on the conduct of the Executive and the
         treaty negotiated by the Chief Justice . . . Philadelphia . . .
         1795. 8vo. 56p., with a variant (signature "B" is printed).

         By Alexander James Dallas?

         Gaines 132a,b. William Cobbett, Works of Peter Porcupine,
         London 1801, Vol. II, p. 355, note, identifies as Dallas.
         Attr. to Eleazer Oswald (its printer) E. 29256; Howes 0138.
         Not attr. S. 101838; Jeff. 3178.

95-27   The letters of Sicilius . . . sale of western lands in the State of
         Georgia . . . By a citizen of that State . . . 1795. 8vo. 66p.
         (also ed. 94p.).

         By James Jackson.

         E. 28889; Vail 1028; Howes J21; Abernethy 151. S.
         27067 not attr.

95-28   Letters on . . . representation in the Legislature of South-
         Carolina . . . by Phocion. Charleston . . . 1795. 8vo. 33p.

         By Henry W. Desaussure.

         E. 28562; S. 87866; Turnbull p. 314; D.A.B. 5:254.

95-29   A letter to the Rev. Jedediah Morse . . . By a Citizen of Wil-
         liamsburg. Richmond . . . 1795. 8vo. 16p.

         By St. George Tucker.

         E. 29662; S. 97378+, saying also attr. to Bishop James
         Madison. Not attr. S. 40517.

95-30   Liberty. A poem, delivered on the Fourth of July . . . by "The
         Stranger" . . . Newburyport. 1795. 8vo. 10p.

         By Isaac Story.

E. 29572; Weg. 379; D.A.B. 18:102.

95-31   A little plain English, addressed to the people of the United
         States, on the Treaty . . . By Peter Porcupine . . . Phila-
         delphia . . . 1795. 8vo. (5)6-8, (1)2-111(1)p; plus two
         variants; also London, same.

         By William Cobbett.

         Gaines 7a-d; E. 28437; S. 13895; S. 101847+; Pearl 8. E.
         28438 indicates a Boston reprint, unknown.

95-32   Mr. Thomas Paine's Trial; being an examination of his Age of
         Reason . . . Boston 1795. 8vo. 79p.

         By Ebenezer Bradford.

         E. 28338.

95-33   A new and easy plan to redeem the American captives in
         Algiers . . . By an American Citizen. Philadelphia 1795.

         By James Leach?

         STE 28956 (entry from copyright notice).

95-34   New Year's verses. For the Connecticut Courant, January 1,
         1795. (Hartford?) 1795. Broadside.

         By Lemuel Hopkins.

         E. 28472. Reprinted in "The Echo" (no. 07-07) pp. 209-
         218.

95-35   Observations on the emigration of Dr. Joseph Priestley . . .
         Farmer's Bull. The Third Edition . . . Philadelphia . . .
         1795. 8vo. 88p.

         By William Cobbett.

         Gaines 2h; E. 28439, 28440. See no. 94-23.

95-36   Part II. A Bone to Gnaw for the Democrats . . . By Peter
         Porcupine . . . Philadelphia . . . 1795. 8vo. (3)iv-viii, 66,
         (2)p., two issues. Also Second Edition . . . (3)iv-vii(1), 66,
         (2)p., three issues.

By William Cobbett.

Gaines 6a-6e; E. 28434, 28435; Pearl 5; S. 13876.

95-37   Plan of association of the North American Land Company . . .
        Philadelphia . . . 1795. 8vo. 25p., leaf.

        By Robert Morris?

        B. Ath. p. 144. Not attr. in E. 29220; S. 55548; Vail 1035.

95-38   Political Observations (caption title; dated April 20, 1795).
        8vo. 24p.

        By James Madison.

        E. 29017; S. 43718; Jeff. 3177; Cronin & Wise, Madison
        85.

95-39   The political progress of Britain . . . Part second . . . Philadel-
        phia . . . 1795. 8vo. iv(1)6-96p.

        By James Thomson Callender.

        S. 10066; E. 28381; Kress B2898; Jeff. 3184. See no.
        94-27.

95-40   Queries respecting the introduction, progress and abolition of
        slavery in Massachusetts. (Boston 1795). Broadside.

        By Jeremy Belknap.

        E. 28257.

95-41   Remarks on the Jacobiniad . . . Boston . . . 1795. 8vo. 54p.
        6 plates.

        By John S. J. Gardiner.

        STE 28726; S. 26623; Weg. 180; Morse 151; D.A.B. 7:138.
        See no. 98-58 for part second.

95-42   A reply to the address . . . George Muter and Benjamin Sebastian
        . . . 1795. 8vo. 31p.

        By Humphrey Marshall.

        E. 29024; A.I.I. 5:49; S. 44778.

95-43   Réponse aux principales questions . . . sur les Etats-Unis de
         l'Amérique, par un citoyen adoptif de la Pensylvanie . . .
         Lausanne . . . 1795. 8vo., 2v., 450, 469p.

         By J. Esprit Bonnet.

         Kress B2890; CHA 18615 2:6; S. 6324, second title, simi-
         lar. Reprinted Paris 1802 under Bonnet S. 6323.

95-44   A Rub from Snub; or a cursory analytical Epistle: addressed
         to Peter Porcupine . . . Philadelphia . . . 1795. 8vo. vi(1)8-
         80p.

         By John Swanwick.

         Gaines 134; E. 29594; CHA 19106 3:3. See note S. 94025+
         (however, this work is confused with no. 96-17). S. 85597
         not attr. S. 14032 attr. to Cobbett, but the work attacks
         Cobbett.

95-45   A short history of the nature and consequences of excise laws
         . . . interruption to the manufactories . . . Phila. . . . 1795.
         8vo. 116p.; two imprints, one "sold in New York".

         By James Thomson Callender.

         E. 28383, 28384; S. 10071; S. 80640; Jeff. 3183.

95-46   The Spirit of Despotism . . . Philadelphia: Re-printed . . . 1795.
         12mo. (10)342p.

         By Vicesimus Knox.

         E. 28936; S. 89471.

95-47   A statement of the cause of the M'Clary owners . . . to its close
         in the Supreme Court . . . Portsmouth . . . 1795. 16mo. 67p.

         By John Hale.

         CHA 17151 1:2; E. 28788; S. 29638.

95-48   Strictures on the love of power in the prelacy . . . veto . . . pro-
         ceedings of the clergy and laity . . . Charleston . . . 1795.
         12mo. 68p.

         By Henry Purcell.

S. 66672; STE 29374.

95-49   A twig of birch for a butting calf, or, strictures . . . emigration
        of Doctor Joseph Priestley . . . New York . . . 1795. 8vo.
        46(2)p.

        By Joseph Priestley?

        Attr. to Priestley in Bulletin, British Association for Ameri-
        can Studies, March 1961, p. 25, note 9 (No. 2, new series).
        Not attr. E. 29665; S. 14000. Not in Crook, Ronald E.,
        A Bibliography of Joseph Priestley, London, 1966.

95-50   A vindication of Mr. Randolph's resignation. Philadelphia . . .
        1795. 8vo. 103p. Nine lines of errata on p.(3); plus a
        variant with † before signature K; plus edition with † before
        signatures, three line note to printer on p.(3).

        By Edmund Jennings Randolph.

        Gaines 133a-c; E. 29384,85; S. 67817, 99797+; Jeff. 3180.

95-51   Vindication of the Treaty (Of amity, etc.). By Curtius. Phila-
        delphia 1795; also second edition, pp. 58-108.

        By Noah Webster, Jr. and by James Kent (nos. v and vi).

        P. 194-275 of E. 29752; Jeff. 505; CHA 11850 3:5. See
        Skeel p. 493, no. 6; p. 494, no. 12, 15. CHA 11850 3:5 is
        2d edition.

95-52   The works of Peter Porcupine D.D. A new edition . . . Phila-
        delphia . . . 1795. Title and five pamphlets.

        By William Cobbett.

        Gaines 9a; Pearl 10.

1796

96-01   Abridgement of the public permanent laws of Virginia . . .
         Richmond . . . 1796. 4to. (2)386p.

         By Edmund Randolph.

         Jeff. 1867. Swem 7853; E. 31497 not attr.

96-02   An Account of the proceedings of the Ilinois and Ouabache
         Land Companies . . . Phila. . . . 1796. 8vo. (16)55, 30;
         also (16)55, 26; also 8p., l., 55p.

         By William Smith, provost.

         S. 34196, 84577; Vail 1089; Howes S684; CHA 21806
         3:5. E. 30618; S. 96 not attr.

96-03   Address from the Roman Catholics of America to George
         Washington . . . London . . . 1796. fol. 8p.

         By John Carroll.

         S. 11071.

96-04   Address to the House of Representatives . . . Lord Grenville's
         Treaty . . . Phila. . . . 1796. 8vo. (5)iv-vi(1)10-46(1) 48p.

         By Mathew Carey.

         STE 29952; E. 30156; B. Ath. p. 42; Rowe 41.

96-05   Address to the people of the congressional district . . . counties
         of Wythe . . . Philadelphia. 1796. 8vo. 29p.

         By Francis Preston.

         E. 31045.

96-06   The adventures of a porcupine . . . genuine memoirs of a no-
         torious rogue . . . By Daniel Detector . . . Phila. . . . 1796.
         8vo. (2)(4)5-47(1)p.; front.

         By A. Henderson.

         Gaines 142; E. 30553; Howes H406 (Howes has "Archibald
         Henderson").

96-07   An antidote for Tom Paine's . . . poison . . . Philadelphia 1796.
        8vo. (3)4-79(1)p.

        By William Cobbett.

        Gaines 20b; E. 30204.

96-08   Between Joseph Wilkins . . . Taylor. (Richmond 1796). 8vo.
        30(1)p. Caption title.

        By George Wythe.

        E. 31670.

96-09   Between William Fowler . . . Saunders. (Richmond 1796). 8vo.
        28p. Caption title.

        By George Wythe.

        E. 31668.

96-10   Between William Yates . . . Salle. (Richmond 1796). 8vo.
        30(1)p. Caption title.

        By George Wythe.

        E. 31671.

96-11   The bible needs no apology . . . a short answer to Paine . . .
        Portsmouth . . . 1796. 8vo. 96p.

        By Daniel Humphreys.

        Jeff. 1653; E. 30603.

96-12   The bloody buoy thrown out as a warning to the political
        pilots of America; . . . By Peter Porcupine . . . Philadelphia
        . . . 1796. 12mo. xii(1)16-241(1)p. 4 plates; plus second
        edition 24mo. xii(1)16-362p. 4 plates; plus same without
        plates; plus same with frontispiece; plus London edition
        without plates.

        By William Cobbett.

        Gaines 12a-e; E. 30205-07; S. 13873; Pearl 14.

96-13   The Blue Shop . . . observations on the Life and adventures of

Peter Porcupine . . . by James Quicksilver. Phila. . . . 1796. 8vo. 52p.

By Santiago Felipe (James Philip) Puglia.

Gaines 146; E. 31065; Clark p. 190. S. 14023 not attr. Attr. to Joseph Scott by Mathew Carey Autobiography, 1833.

96-14   A bone to gnaw, for the democrats . . . by Peter Porcupine . . . The fourth edition . . . Philadelphia . . . 1796. 8vo. (3)iv-vi(1)2-66p

By William Cobbett.

Gaines 3e; the third title in E. 30234. See no. 95-05.

96-15   Bradford's fourth edition. Observations on the emigration of Dr. Joseph Priestley . . . Philadelphia . . . 1796 . . . 8vo. 88p.

By William Cobbett.

Gaines 2i; E. 30218. See no. 96-42.

96-16   A Brief consideration of the important services . . . recommend Mr. Adams for the presidency . . . Boston . . . 1796. (by Aurelius). 8vo. 31p.

By John Gardner.

E. 30472; S. 26649; Cronin & Wise, Adams 149; Du Puy 940. Entry repeated STE 34116 under John Gardner Milton.

96-17   British honour and humanity . . . applause of Mr. William Cobbet [sic] . . . by a friend to regular government. Philadelphia . . . 1796. 8vo. 58p.

By James Thomson Callender.

Gaines 137. Cobbett pointed to Callender in E. 30727, p. 94. Clark p. 190: "Probably by J. T. Callender, as Cobbett thought". Jeff. 3185 has "T. Callendar". Attr. to John Swanwick in E. 31255; S. 94022+. Howes C515 suggests Mathew Carey. S. 8110 not attr.

96-18   Case upon the statute for distribution . . . Richmond . . . 1796.
         8vo. 38p. Caption title.

         By George Wythe.

         E. 31672. Swem 823 not attr.

96-19   Cautionary hints to Congress respecting the sale of the western
         lands . . . second edition . . . Phila. 1796. 8vo. 13(3)p.

         By Colonel James Wood?

         See no. 95-08. S. 105034 suggests Wood. E. 30254; S.
         11587 not attr. Kress B3107 "ascribed to St. George
         Tucker".

96-20   A Congratulatory epistle to the redoubtable "Peter Porcupine"
         . . . by Peter Grievous, Junr. . . . Phila. . . . 1796. 8vo. 44p.

         By Joseph Hopkinson?

         Gaines 143; CHA 5083 1:4. STE 30593; S. 14025 not attr.
         (However, S. 32980 identifies Peter Grievous as Francis Hopkin-
         son, who was Joseph's father.) Weg. 528 not attr.

96-21   A description of the River Susquehanna, . . . trade and naviga-
         tion . . . Phila. . . . 1796. 8vo. (4)60p. map.

         By Jonathan Williams Condy?

         Vail 1059; S. 93935; Howes C669. STE 30338 (with "?").
         Wheat 311.

96-22   Des Prisons de Philadelphie. Par un Européen. Phila. . . . 1796.
         8vo. 44p. Also Paris, 63p.; Amsterdam.

         By La Rochefoucauld-Liancourt.

         E. 30673; Monaghan 916-9; S. 39053 (Paris); S. 39055
         (Amsterdam). S. 50576 mistakenly attr. to Moreau de Saint-
         Méry. See no. 96-43.

96-23   The Federalist . . . strictures upon a pamphlet entitled "The
         pretensions of Thomas Jefferson . . ." Philadelphia . . . 1796.
         8vo. 48p.; Ditto, Part the second, same place and date, 8vo.
         27p.

By Tench Coxe.

E. 30293, 30294; Malone 3 p. 282 note; CHA 5418 2:3.
Not attr. Tompk. Jeff. 67, Johnston 26 or S. 23994.

96-24   The foresters, an American tale; being a sequel to the history of
         John Bull the clothier . . . second edition . . . Boston . . .
         1796. 8vo., x, l., 12-240p.

         By Jeremy Belknap.

         E. 30051; CHA 2040 1:1; S. 4433. See no. 92-16.

96-25   The Gros mousqueton diplomatique . . . citizen Adet . . . pref-
         ace by Peter Porcupine. Phila. . . . 1796. 8vo. (5)iv-vi(1)6-72p.

         By William Cobbett.

         Gaines 23; E. 30208; S. 13884; Pearl 22.

96-26   The Group: or an elegant representation . . . Phila. . . . 1796.
         4to. 35(1)p. plate.

         By William Cliffton.

         E. 30202; S. 13695; Weg. 75; D.A.B. 4:219. Not attr. in
         S. 28977.

96-27   The Guillotina, or a democratic dirge, a poem. By the author
         of the "Democratiad" . . . Philadelphia (1796). 8vo. 8p.;
         also 14p.

         By Lemuel Hopkins.

         E. 30590, 30591; Weg. 205; CHA 8689 2:3; D.A.B. 9:215.
         S. 13885 erroneously attr. to William Cobbett. See B.A.L.
         1:178 (Barlow). Texts same as next item and are probably
         later reprints.

96-28   Guillotina; or the Annual Song of the tenth muse . . . broadside.
         44.5x24.5cm. Caption title, three columns, dated at foot:
         Hartford. January 1, 1796.

         By Lemuel Hopkins.

         E. 30269; Howard p. 201. Reprinted in the Echo, no. 07-07,
         and noted as "principally written by a late eminent physician

in Connecticut." Hopkins, who practiced medicine, died 1801. See preceding item.

96-29 He wou'd be a poet . . . epistle on electioneering success. By Geoffrey Touchstone. Phila. . . . 1796. 8vo. 28p.

By James Carey.

Gaines 139; E. 30154; Weg. 53; Clark p. 84, 190.

96-30 History of the American Jacobins, commonly denominated Democrats. By Peter Porcupine . . . Philadelphia . . . 1796. 8vo. (5)8-48p.; plus possibly an edition of Dec. 1796.

By William Cobbett.

Gaines 24d, e; E. 30209. This was an appendix to E. 31016, "The History of Jacobinism . . . 1796." The preliminary leaf, missing in the separate copies, has "AP-PENDIX" on the recto.

96-31 The impostor detected, or a review of some of the writings of Peter Porcupine . . . Philadelphia 1796. 8vo. xvii(2)20-51(3)3-23(1)p.; plus second edition, same.

By Samuel F. Bradford.

Gaines 136a, b; E. 30119,20. S. 14026 not attr.

96-32 A kick for a bite . . . second edition . . . Philadelphia . . . 1796. 8vo. (5)6-31(1)p.; plus a variant.

By William Cobbett.

Gaines 4c, d; E. 30210. See no. 95-24.

96-33 The Lay preacher; or short sermons, for idle readers. . . . Walpole . . . 1796. 12mo. 132p.

By Joseph Dennie.

E. 30335; S. 19585.

96-34 Letters of Helvidius: Written in reply to Pacificus, on the President's Proclamation of Neutrality . . . Phila. . . . 1796. 8 vo. 48p.

By James Madison.

E. 30734; Ford 62; Jeff. 3170; Howes M200.

96-35   Letters of Pacificus . . . Proclamation of Neutrality . . . Phila.
         . . . 1796. 8vo. 60(1)p.

By Alexander Hamilton.

E. 30533; S. 29967, 101839; Ford 60; Jeff. 3169;
Howes H119. Reprinted 1802 S. 23981.

96-36   A letter to George Washington . . . strictures on his address . . .
         By Jasper Dwight of Vermont . . . Philadelphia . . . 1796.
         8vo. 48p. On thick or on thin paper.

By William Duane (or his workman, Treziulney).

Attr. to Duane in STE 31315; S. 20989; Jeff. 3192, and
Gilman p. 79. Duane favored in Howes D515. Treziulney
favored in E. 31315, E. 32940 (note) and S. 96800. See
E. 35272, "Plumb Pudding", etc., p. 24, where Mathew
Carey attr. to Duane. In his autobiography (1833) Carey
attr. to Treziulney. See no. 97-29.

96-37   The life and adventures of Peter Porcupine . . . make a fortune
         by writing pamphlets. By Peter Porcupine himself . . .
         Philadelphia . . . 1796. 8vo. viii(1)10-58(2)p.; plus a
         variant; also second edition viii(1)10-56p.

By William Cobbett.

Gaines 19a-c; E. 30212,13; S. 13892; Pearl 17.

96-38   A little plain English . . . on the treaty . . . second edition . . .
         Philadelphia . . . 1796. 8vo. (5)4,5(2)2-77(3)p.; plus a
         variant.

By William Cobbett.

Gaines 7e, f; E. 30214. See no. 95-31.

96-39   Love against Donelson . . . (Richmond 1796). 8vo. 34p. Cap-
         tion title.

By George Wythe.

E. 31669.

96-40   A New-year's gift to the Democrats . . . Mr. Randolph's resigna-
         tion. By Peter Porcupine . . . Philadelphia . . . 1796. 8vo.
         (3)iv(1)6-71(1)p., with two variants; also second edition,
         same, with three variants.

         By William Cobbett.

         Gaines 10a-g; E. 30215; S. 13896; Pearl 12; Howes C522.

96-41   Observations on Mr. Buckminster's sermon . . . duty of repub-
         lican citizens, in the choice of their rulers . . . Portsmouth
         . . . 1796. 8vo. 23p.

         By Daniel Humphreys?

         STE 30606 with question mark. S. 8931 not attr.

96-42   Observations on the emigration of Dr. Joseph Priestley . . .
         1796. Philadelphia. 8vo. (3)4-64p.

         By William Cobbett.

         Gaines 2j; S. 13899; E. 30217. See no. 94-23.

96-43   On the prisons of Philadelphia. By an European. Philadelphia
         . . . 1796. 8vo. 46(2)p.

         By La Rochefoucauld-Liancourt.

         E. 30674; S. 39054; Roberts 179; Monaghan 920. S.
         50577 mistakenly attr. to Moreau de Saint-Méry. See no.
         96-22.

96-44   A Pill for Porcupine: being a specific for an obstinate itching
         . . . By a friend to political equality . . . Phila. . . . 1796.
         8vo. iv(1)6-83(1)p.

         By James Carey.

         Gaines 138; E. 30155; and Clark p. 190. S. 14029 not
         attr.

96-45   A poem, on reading President Washington's address, declining
         a re-election to the presidency. By S. J. H. . . . Albany
         (1796). 8vo. 8p.

         By St. John Honeywood.

         E. 30579; S. 32784; Weg. 202. Reprinted in his "Poems"
         (1801), S. 32786.

96-46   A poem on reading the President's address; with a sketch of the
         character of a candidate for the presidency. Philadelphia
         . . . 1796. 8vo. 7p.

         By St. John Honeywood.

         E. 30580; Weg. 202; S. 63587, 101872+. Not attr. Weg.
         729.

96-47   No entry

96-48   The political censor (for March) . . . By Peter Porcupine . . .
         Philadelphia 1796. 8vo. (3)iv-vi(3)8-70p.; plus second
         edition 8vo. (3)4-6(1)8-70p.; plus third edition 8vo. (5)
         38-104p.

         By William Cobbett.

         Gaines 13a-c; E. 30219,20.

96-49   The political censor (for April) . . . By Peter Porcupine . . .
         Philadelphia 1796. 8vo., plate, (5)72-158, 158-165, 167-
         169(1)p.; plus a variant; plus second edition, 8vo., plate,
         (5)106-169(1)p.; plus same (7)106-169(1)p.; plus third
         edition 8vo., plate, (5)106-169(1)p.; plus a variant.

         By William Cobbett.

         Gaines 14a-f; E. 30221, 22.

96-50   The political censor (for May) . . . By Peter Porcupine . . .
         Philadelphia 1796. 8vo., plate, (5)173-239p.; plus a
         variant; plus second edition, 8vo., (5)174-240p.; plus third

edition, same; plus a variant.

By William Cobbett.

Gaines 17a-e; E. 30223, 24.

96-51   The political censor (for September) . . . By Peter Porcupine . . .
         Philadelphia 1796. 8vo. (3)4-79(1)p.

         By William Cobbett.

         Gaines 20a; E. 30225.

96-52   The political massacre, . . . writings of our present scribblers.
         By James Quicksilver . . . Phila. . . . 1796. 8vo. 29(3)p.,
         folded plate.

         By Santiago Felipe (James Philip) Puglia.

         Gaines 147; E. 31066. S. 67166 not attr.

96-53   Political Truth . . . inquiry . . . charges preferred against Mr.
         Randolph. Phila. . . . 1796. 8vo. 44p.

         By Edmund Jennings Randolph.

         E. 31072; S. 67815; Jeff. 3186; Howes R54.

96-54   The Political wars of Otsego: or downfall of Jacobinism and
         despotism . . . By the author of the Plough-Jogger. Coopers-
         town . . . 1796. 8vo. 122(4)p.

         By Jedidiah Peck.

         E. 30968; S. 59477; Howes P168; Smith 391n.

96-55   Porcupine's political censor, for November 1796 . . . Phila-
         delphia . . . 1796. 8vo. (5)6-78(2)p.; plus a variant.

         By William Cobbett.

         Gaines 25a, b; E. 30226.

96-56   Presidents march . . . New York (1796?). Fol. 1 leaf.

         By Philip File.

STE 31044.

96-57   President II. Being observations on the late official address of
          George Washington. (Philadelphia) 1796. 16p. 8vo.; also
          Baltimore, same; Newark, same.

          By Samuel Relf and James Armstrong Neal.

          Proceedings of the American Antiquarian Society, Vol. 75,
          p. 240. Not attr. in E. 31042,43; STE 47885; E. Supp.
          B9664; S. 65343, 101873.

96-58   The pretensions of Thomas Jefferson to the presidency ex-
          amined; and the charges against John Adams refuted . . .
          1796. Signed, Phocion. (First part). 8vo. 64p.

          By William Loughton Smith (assisted by Oliver Wolcott).

          E. 31212; S. 84831; Jeff. 3174; D.A.B. 17:365; Rogers
          292.

96-59   The pretensions of Thomas Jefferson to the presidency ex-
          amined; and the charges against John Adams refuted . . .
          Part the second . . . 1796. 8vo. (2)42p.

          By William Loughton Smith (assisted by Oliver Wolcott).
          Appendix: Vindication of Mr. Adams's Defence of the
          American Constitutions. Signed, Union. By William Vans
          Murray.

          E. 31213; S. 84832, 104983+; Jeff. 3174. See Dauer, p.
          100-101.

96-60   The probationary odes of Jonathan Pindar esq. a cousin of
          Peter's . . . Philadelphia . . . 1796. 12mo. 103p.

          By St. George Tucker.

          E. 31320; S. 97380; Jeff. 4511; Bryan 151,2; D.A.B.
          19:39; Weg. 407; Davis 330. Attr. to Philip Freneau in
          S. 62911. Paltsits p. 71 is convinced it is not by Freneau.
          Accord, B.A.L. 3:255; Leary, "that rascal Freneau", 235.

96-61   A Prospect from the Congress-gallery during the session, begun
          December 7, 1795 . . . By Peter Porcupine. Philadelphia . . .

1796. 8vo. (3)iv(1)2-12; 17-68p. Also second edition, (3)iv(1)2-64p.

By William Cobbett.

Gaines 11a, b; E. 30229, 30230; S. 14010; Pearl 13.

96-62   The reign of felicity, being a plan for civilizing the Indians of North America . . . London . . . 1796. 12mo. 12p.

By Thomas Spence.

S. 89288. S. 69102 not attr.

96-63   Remarks on the bill of rights . . . State of Virginia . . . By a Virginian born and bred. (n.p.) 1796. 35p.

By James Hay.

STE 47801. E. 30549 gives Richmond imprint, but its origin is unknown.

96-64   Remarks on the treaty . . . concluded between lord Grenville and mr. Jay . . . By a citizen of the United States. Phila. . . . 1796 (signed Columbus). 8vo. 36p.

By St. George Tucker?

Davis p. 401. E. 30255 not attr.; but see no. 95-08.

96-65   A Reply to the False Reasoning in the "Age of Reason" . . . By a Layman. Philadelphia . . . 1796. 12mo. 40p.

By Miers Fisher.

E. 30423; Jeff. 1654.

96-66   A report of the case between Field and Harrison . . . Richmond . . . 1796. 8vo. 32p. (caption title).

By George Wythe.

E. 31667.

96-67   The revelation of nature, with the prophesy of reason . . . New York (1796). 12mo., xxxix, (1)104p.

By John Stewart.

CHA 20818 1:5; E. 31238.

96-68   Review of the events and treaties . . . balance of trade in favor
        of Great Britain . . . (London?) 1796. 2p., l., 181p., fold.
        map.

        By John Bruce.

        Kress B3102; Edinburgh 1:563.

96-69   A Roaster; or, a check to the progress of political blasphemy
        . . . reply to Peter Porcupine . . . by Sim Sansculotte.
        Phila. . . . 1796. 8vo. (3)4-21(3)p.

        By John Swanwick.

        Gaines 150; E. 31256; S. 94025 note; Clark p. 81, 190.
        S. 14031 attr. to William Cobbett, but it attacks him.

96-70   The Scare-crow; being an infamous letter . . . By Peter Porcu-
        pine. Philadelphia . . . 1796. 8vo. (3)4-23(1)p., plus a
        variant. Also second edition, same.

        By William Cobbett.

        Gaines 18a-c; E. 30231, 30232; S. 14016; Pearl 16.

96-71   A sermon for December 15, 1796 . . . public thanksgiving . . .
        Boston . . . 1796. 8vo. 21p.

        By James Freeman.

        E. 30451; S. 25765.

96-72   A Short description of the State of Tennessee . . . Phila. . . .
        1796. 12mo. 44p. Also "Tennassee", 36p., map.

        By Daniel Smith.

        E. 31199, 31200; S. 82421, 82422, 94805+; Jeff. 3541;
        Howes S587. See no. 93-30.

96-73   Sketches on . . . crops . . . manufactures . . . sources of trade,
        interfering . . . in foreign markets. Philadelphia . . . 1796.
        8vo. (2)76p.

By John Beale Bordley.

E. 30103. See nos. 94-15 and 97-60.

96-74   The South-Carolina justice of peace . . . second edition . . .
        Philadelphia . . . 1796. 8vo. viii641(2)p.

        By John F. Grimké.

        E. 30519.

96-75   The Susquehannah title stated and examined . . . Printed in
        Catskill by Mackay Croswell. 1796. 8vo. 115p., folding
        insert (STE).

        By Barnabas Bidwell.

        STE 30091; S. 93937; Howes B431; Vail 1050; Streeter
        982.

96-76   Third Edition. The Democratiad, a poem in retaliation . . .
        By a Gentleman of Connecticut. Philadelphia . . . 1796.
        8vo. 22(1)p.

        By Lemuel Hopkins.

        E. 30589. See no. 95-13.

96-77   Tit for tat; or, a purge for a pill . . . By Dick Retort. (1796).
        8vo. (3)iv, v(2)8-34; (3)4-25(1)p.

        By Benjamin Davies.

        Gaines 141; E. 30314; Clark 75, 100. Attr. to Davies by
        Mathew Carey in E. 30160. S. 95866+ suggests Davies. S.
        14018 and STE 30314 attr. to William Cobbett. Not Pearl.
        The second portion "A poetical rhapsody on the times", is
        attr. to William Cliffton E. 30314; D.A.B. 4:219; S.
        70130+.

96-78   The unmasked nabob of Hancock County: or, the scales dropt
        from the eyes of the people. Portsmouth . . . 1796. 8vo.
        (9)11-24p.

        By Samuel Ely.

New England Quarterly Vol. v(1932) 105-134, Robert E.
Moody; Henry Knox, by North Callahan, New York, Rine-
hart & Co., Inc., 1958, pp. 353,4. Not attr. S. 98021; E.
31477. The "nabob" was Knox.

96-79   The works of Peter Porcupine, D.D. . . . Philadelphia . . . 1796.
Title and six pamphlets, varying editions.

By William Cobbett.

Gaines 9b-d; Pearl 10.

96-80   The works of Peter Porcupine. Fourth edition. Philadelphia
1796. Title and five pamphlets.

By William Cobbett.

Gaines 9e; E. 30234.

1797

97-01   An account of a new poorhouse . . . Philadelphia . . . 1797.
8vo. 23p.

By William Gilpin.

E. 32194.

97-02   The Algerine captive . . . Walpole . . . 1797. 12mo., 2 vols.
214, 241p.

By Royall Tyler.

E. 32945; S. 97615; D.A.B. 19:97.

97-03   The American annual register, or, historical memoirs of the
United States, for the year 1796. Phila. . . . 1797. 8vo.
vii(1)288p.; plus a variant.

By James Thomson Callender.

Gaines 151a, b; E. 31905; S. 10062; Howes C69; D.A.B.
3:425.

97-04   The American Gazetteer, or Geographical Companion . . . New
         York . . . 1797. 12mo., 54p., map.

         By Charles Smith.

         CHA 709 1:7; E. 32841.

97-05   Annals of blood . . . by an American . . . Cambridge (England)
         . . . 1797. 12mo. (2)iii(2)2-154(2)p.

         By William Cobbett.

         Gaines 12h; S. 13874+. See no. 96-12.

97-06   Anticipation! Peter Porcupine's descent into hell . . . By Henry
         Hedgehog . . . second edition . . . Philadelphia . . . 1797. 8vo.
         8p.

         By James Carey.

         Gaines 152; E. 31914; Clark p. 104.

97-07   The Antigallican; or, the lover of his own country . . . By a
         Citizen of New England. Philadelphia . . . 1797. 8vo. (5)6-
         71, 71, 73(2)74-82p.; also (5)6-69, 67, 71-73(2)74-82p.

         By John Lowell.

         Gaines 109a, b; E. 32393; S. 42444+; Howes L528; Cronin
         & Wise, Adams 165; Johnston, p. 26. Not attr. in S. 1691.

97-08   Biographical, literary and political anecdotes . . . persons of the
         present age . . . London 1797. 8vo. 3 vols.

         By John Almon.

         S. 950.

97-09   The bloody buoy . . . third edition . . . London . . . 1797. 12mo.
         xvi, 259(1)p.

         By William Cobbett.

         Gaines 12g; Pearl 14.

97-10   A bone to gnaw for the Democrats . . . third edition . . . Phila-
         delphia . . . 1797. 8vo. (3)iv, v(2)41, 3-66p.; also (3)92, 93(2)

96-160p.

By William Cobbett.

Gaines 3f, g; E. 31945.

97-11   A bone to gnaw for the Democrats. By Peter Porcupine . . . a
         rod, for the back of the critics . . . London . . . 1797. 12mo.,
         1p., l., xcv, l., v., l., 8-175 (really 177) (1)p., l.; plus a variant.

         By William Cobbett.

         Gaines 3h, 3i; CHA 2472 3:7; S. 64161.

97-12   The carriers of Porcupine's Gazette . . . (Philadelphia 1797).
         Broadside, 36.6x27cm.

         By William Cobbett.

         Gaines 35; E. 34400 (1798).

97-13   The case of the Georgia sales on the Mississippi considered . . .
         Philadelphia . . . 1797. 8vo. (2)109p.; also (4)109p.

         By Robert G. Harper.

         STE 48138, 35588; E. Supp. B9956; Howes H208; Brin.
         3930; Turnbull 337. Signed on p. 58.

97-14   The case of the manufacturers of soap and candles, in the City
         of New York . . . New York 1797. 8vo. 62p.

         By Samuel L. Mitchill.

         STE 32564; S. 49737; Austin 90; Kress B3468. Not attr.
         in E. 32564.

97-15   The deformity of a hideous monster, discovered in the Province
         of Maine, by a man in the woods, looking after liberty.
         (Boston 1797). 8vo. 31p.

         By Samuel Ely.

         E. 32081; S. 22388 (12p.). See no. 96-78.

97-16   Die blut-fahne (bloody buoy) . . . Reading (Pa.) 1797. 8vo.
         (12)198(2)p. 4 plates.

By William Cobbett.

Gaines 12f; E. 31944. See no. 96-12.

97-17   The disappointment, or Peter Porcupine in London . . . by
         James Quicksilver . . . Philadelphia . . . 1797.

         By Santiago Felipe (James Philip) Puglia?

         STE 32731. No copy known. See Gaines 146.

97-18   The duty of executors and administrators . . . New York 1797.
         8vo., (xvii) 343(2)p., two tables.

         By John F. Grimké.

         E. 32214.

97-19   An examination of the conduct of the executive of the United
         States . . . French Republic . . . By a citizen of Pennsylvania
         . . . Philadelphia . . . 1797. 8vo. vi, 72p.

         By Albert Gallatin.

         E. 32172; S. 26388; B. Ath. 84; Swem 1906; CHA 4514
         3:6; D.A.B. 7:103.

97-20   A few observations on some late public transactions . . . Con-
         gress . . . election for a chief magistrate . . . Charleston 1797.
         Signed, A Steady Federalist. 8vo. 27p.

         By Christopher Gadsden.

         E. 32168; Turnbull p. 335.

97-21   A five minutes answer to Paine's letter to General Washington
         . . . London 1797. 8vo. 2p.l.(1)4-44p.

         By Charles L. P. Horry.

         CHA 7161 1:7; Howes H649; B. Ath. p. 520.

97-22   Guillotina, for 1797 . . . Hartford . . . 1797. Fol. p(2); also
         broadside (Philadelphia?).

         By Lemuel Hopkins.

         E. 31978, 31979. See no. 96-28.

97-23   The history of Jack Nips. Walpole. (N.H.) 1797. 15p., 17cm.

By John Leland.

STE 48165. See nos. 92-17, 93-14, 94-37. Not attr. E.
Supp. B9964.

97-24   History of the American Jacobins, commonly denominated
Democrats. By Peter Porcupine . . . Edinburgh . . . Jan.
1797. 12mo. (3)iv, (1)6-47(1)p.

By William Cobbett.

Gaines 24f; CHA 11356 2:6. See no. 96-30 for American
edition.

97-25   The History of the United States for 1796 . . . Philadelphia
. . . 1797. 8vo. viii, 312p.

By James Thomson Callender.

E. 31906; S. 10064; Ford 67; Jeff. 3515.

97-26   A letter to the infamous Tom Paine . . . Washington . . .
(Philadelphia 1797?). 8vo. (1)2-18(2)p.; also London
1797 8vo. (5)6-23(1)p.; plus Glasgow 1797 12mo.
(5)6-24p.; plus a variant. Caption title.

By William Cobbett.

Gaines 26e-h; Pearl 24; S. 101837. Taken from December Political Censor, no. 97-44.

97-27   The Letters of Fabius, in 1788 . . . and in 1797 on the present
situation of public affairs . . . Wilmington . . . 1797. 8vo.
iv, 202p. l.

By John Dickinson.

CHA 6115 2:7; E. 32042; Cush. 1p. 98; Howes D330.

97-28   Letters of Verus, addressed to the native American. Philadelphia . . . 1797. 8vo. vi, 75p.

By Carlos Martinez de Yrujo.

S. 106216. Also attr. to Philip Fatio, secretary to Yrujo.

Name confused in E. 33259. Attr. to Yrujo by Timothy Pickering: "Message from the President . . . Missisippi . . . 23d January 1798 . . ." p. 9. Authorship acknowledged by Yrujo, see Roberts, p. 244. Wandell p. 19 attr. to John Armstrong. See Dauer p. 361; Howes Y36.

97-29   Letter to George Washington . . . strictures on his address . . . By Jasper Dwight of Vermont . . . Baltimore . . . 1797. 12mo. 44p.

By William Duane (or his workman Treziulney).

STE 32940; Minick 356. S. 96800 (Treziulney). Cobbett's Porcupine's Gazette July 21, 1797 attr. to Duane. See no. 96-36.

97-30   Lettres de Verus, adressées au native American. (Philadelphia 1797?). 8vo. vi, 68p.

By Carlos Martinez de Yrujo.

S. 106217; E. 33260.

97-31   The life and adventures of Peter Porcupine . . . London 1797 . . . 12mo. (5)iv, v, iv, vii-ix(2)2-58(2)p.; plus a variant.

By William Cobbett.

Gaines 19d, e. See no. 96-37.

97-32   The life of Thomas Paine . . . London . . . 1797. 12mo. (3)4-60p.; also London (1797?) 16mo. (3)2-57(1)p.

By William Cobbett.

Gaines 20d, f; S. 13894. E. Supp. B9897; STE 48090 (no copy located) suggest a Philadelphia edition 1797, but I doubt it.

97-33   Memorial of the Illinois and Wabash Land companies . . . (Philadelphia 1797). 8vo. 8, 8, 7, 7p.; also 26p.

By William Smith, provost.

S. 84577 note; Howes S694. Not attr. E. 32976,77; S. 34294.

97-34   Notes of a few decisions . . . courts . . . North Carolina . . . New-
         bern 1797. (8)78, 83(8)p.

         By François X. Martin.

         E. Supp. B9995; STE 48173. See E. 32426.

97-35   Observations on the debates of the American Congress . . . By
         Peter Porcupine . . . London 1797. 8vo. (3)2-38p.; plus a
         variant.

         By William Cobbett.

         Gaines 26j, k; S. 13897, 101860+; Pearl 27.

97-36   Observations on the emigration of Dr. Joseph Priestley . . .
         farmer's bull . . . (Philadelphia 1797). 8vo. 88p.

         By William Cobbett.

         Gaines 2k; E. 28440 (has 1795).

97-37   An open letter on the position of France since the Jay treaty
         . . . Philadelphia . . . 1797. fol. 2p.

         By Matthew Clay.

         E. 31941.

97-38   Opinions respecting the commercial intercourse . . . Great-
         Britain . . . By a Citizen of Massachusetts . . . Boston . . .
         1797. 8vo. 61(1)p.

         By James Bowdoin.

         E. 31857; S. 7015; Kress B3351; D.A.B. 2:502.

97-39   Part II. A bone to gnaw for the Democrats . . . By Peter
         Porcupine . . . Philadelphia . . . 1797. 8vo. (2)(1)2-66p.;
         two issues.

         By William Cobbett.

         Gaines 6f, g; E. Supp. B9898. "Memoires" and "Memoirs".
         Differ from edition included in E. 31948. See no. 95-36.

97-40   A poem on the President's farewell address, with a sketch of

the character of his successor. Second edition. Philadelphia
... (1797?). 8vo. 8p.

By St. John Honeywood.

STE 48146; S. 63588; E. Supp. B9967; Dex. 4:221. See
no. 96-47; no. 00-39.

97-41   The political reformer ... laws ... United States ... Strictures
         on John Adams's Defence of the Constitutions of govern-
         ment ... (signed Camillus). Phila. ... 1797. 8vo. 73p., l.

         By Michael Forrest.

         E. 32140; Howes F266; CHA 3428 1:1. S. 63799 suggests
         Alexander Hamilton; E. 31909 is corrected by E. 32140.

97-42   Porcupine's political censor, for April 1797 (i.e., 1796) ... by
         Peter Porcupine ... (Philadelphia 1797). 8vo. (5)68-134(2)p.

         By William Cobbett.

         Gaines 14g.

97-43   Porcupine's political censor for Sept. 1796 ... Philadelphia
         (1797). 8vo. (3)252-327(1)p.

         By William Cobbett.

         Gaines 20c; E. 31948.

97-44   Porcupine's political censor for December 1796 ... Philadelphia
         (1797). 8vo. (5)6-47(2)2-18(6)p.; plus a variant; plus
         second edition, 8vo. (3)4-64p.; plus a variant.

         By William Cobbett.

         Gaines 26a-d; E. 30227,28.

97-45   Porcupine's political censor, for Jan. 1797 ... Philadelphia
         (1797). 8vo. (5)4-51(3)p.

         By William Cobbett.

         Gaines 29; E. 31946.

97-46   Porcupine's political censor, for March 1797 ... Philadelphia

(1797). 8vo. (4)53-115(9)p.; plus three variants.

By William Cobbett.

Gaines 31a-d; E. 31947.

97-47   Porcupine's political tracts, of 1794 and 1795 . . . Philadelphia
        . . . 1797. Title and seven pamphlets.

By William Cobbett.

Gaines 33.

97-48   Porcupine's works. Vol. I . . . Philadelphia (1797) . . . 8vo.
        Two leaves and seven pamphlets; plus six variants.

By William Cobbett.

Gaines 27a, b; 34a-e.

97-49   Porcupine's works. Vol. II . . . Philadelphia . . . 1796 (i.e., 1797).
        8vo. two leaves and eight pamphlets; plus four variants.

By William Cobbett.

Gaines 28, 34f-i.

97-50   The Present state of medical learning in the city of New York . . .
        New York . . . 1797. 8vo. 16p.

By Samuel L. Mitchill.

E. 32488; Austin 1322; S. 49749+.

97-51   Queries selected . . . agriculture . . . with answers . . . (Phila-
        delphia 1797). 8vo. 16p.; also 19p.

By John Beale Bordley.

E. 31845 (16p.); Kress B3347 (19p.).

97-52   The Recantation; being an anticipated valedictory address of
        Thomas Paine . . . New-York . . . 1797. 8vo. 15p.; also
        North Carolina 1797 13p.

By Donald Fraser.

E. 32153; see 5 A.I.I. 73. NYPL 1200; E. Supp. B9932;
STE 48118 is North Carolina reprint.

97-53   Reflections on the proposition . . . canal . . . Chesapeake . . .
         Delaware Bay . . . Annapolis . . . (1797). 8vo. 50p.

         By James Carroll.

         STE 32744; Minick 347. S. 68712 not attr.

97-54   Remarks occasioned by the late conduct of mr. Washington,
         as president of the United States . . . Phila. . . . 1797. 8vo.
         iv, 84p.

         By Benjamin Franklin Bache?

         E. 31759; S. 101878 (noting E.). Not attr. STE 31759;
         CHA 18556 3:7; S. 69388; Jeff. 3190; D.A.B. 1:463.

97-55   Review of the Administration . . . since the year ninety-three
         . . . Boston . . . 1797. 8vo. 87p.

         By Timothy Pickering.

         E. 33066; S. 70219; Howes P341.

97-56   Rules for conducting business in the Senate. (Phila. 1797).
         8vo. 7p.

         By Thomas Jefferson.

         E. 33043; cf. S. 74090 (1801).

97-57   A short description of the State of Tennessee . . . New York
         . . . 1797. 47p. 17cm.

         By Daniel Smith.

         STE 48254; E. Supp. B10104; Howes S. 587. See no.
         96-72.

97-58   Short history of the yellow fever . . . in the city of Phila-
         delphia . . . Phila. . . . 1797. 8vo. (1)2-37, 46-64(16)p.

         By Richard Folwell.

         E. 32138; Austin 781. S. 62241 not attr.

97-59   Sketches of French and English politicks in America in May,
         1797. By a member of the Old Congress. Charleston . . .

1797. 8vo., 1p., l., 65p.

By Richard Beresford.

E. 31803; Turnbull p. 334; CHA 2108 3:6. S. 81559 not attr.

97-60   Sketches on . . . crops . . . manufactures . . . sources of trade . . . interfering . . . in foreign markets. Philadelphia. 1797. 8vo. (2)76p.

By John Beale Bordley.

STE 31846; Kress S. 5536. S. 81583 not attr. See no. 96-73.

97-61   To the honourable General Assembly of . . . Connecticut . . . memorial . . . in behalf of ourselves and the poor black people of our nation . . . n.p. (1797) 8vo. 12p.

By Isaac Hilliard.

E. Supp. B9962; Trumb. 2246; STE 32252. This may be STE 48142.

97-62   Twenty thousand muskets!!! Particulars of the capture of the Ship Olive Branch . . . London 1797. 8vo. (4)106p.

By Ira Allen.

S. 823, 97535; Rich 1:402; Howes A145; Gilman p. 8.

97-63   Verses occasioned . . . Answer of the President . . . Treaty with Great Britain. Boston . . . 1797. 16mo. 1(7)p.

By Jonathan M. Sewall.

E. 32823; S. 79402; Weg. 353.

1798

98-01   Adams and liberty . . . (Boston 1798). Broadside, two editions; (Worcester 1798), broadside; also 2 leaves.

By Robert Treat Paine.

E. 34295,96; STE 48557, 48558 (Worcester); E. Supp. B10451, 52,54a.

98-02   Adams and Washington . . . Boston (1798). Broadside.

By Robert Treat Paine.

E. 34300.

98-03   An Address to my influential neighbours . . . Brimfield . . . '98. 8vo. 15(1)p.

By William Eaton.

E. 33662.

98-04   An address to the people of Maryland . . . French aggression . . . by a member of the House of Representatives. Phila. . . . 1798. 8vo. (3)4-76 (i.e., 75); (2)ii-ivp.

By John Dennis or William Hindman.

Attr. to Dennis E. 33626; Howes D253; attr. to Hindman CHA 6006 1:3; E. 35619. Attr. to L. P. Dennis in S. 45064; Brin. 8515, but he was born 1784.

98-05   An Address to the people of Virginia . . . alien and sedition laws. By a Citizen of this State. Richmond . . . 1798. 12mo.(?) 63(1)ivp.

By Thomas Evans.

E. 33702; S. 100425; Swem 7924; Brin. 3717; B. Ath. p. 77; Howes E228.

98-06   An appeal to the candid, upon the present state of religion and politics in Connecticut. (1798). 12mo. 24p.; also 12mo. 16p.

By John C. Ogden.

Dex. 5:316; B. Ath. p. 152; Purcell p. 434; Fisher p. 59.
E. 31739 has New Haven 1797 without attribution; E.
34267 is Litchfield 1798; E. 36454 is 1799 and suggests
Benjamin Trumbull, as does S. 97176 and Trumb. 1872.

98-07   The bloody buoy . . . fourth edition . . . London . . . 1798.
         12mo. xvi,259p.

         By William Cobbett.

         Gaines 12i.

98-08   The bloody buoy, abridged . . . London . . . 1798. 12mo.
         (3)4-24p.

         By William Cobbett.

         Gaines 12j.

98-09   A Caution; or, Reflections on the present contest between
         France and Great Britain . . . (Phila.) 1798. 8vo. 14p.

         By John Dickinson?

         STE 33647. Attr. to William Duane E. 33647; Jeff. 3211.
         Not attr. S. 11586.

98-10   Circular letter. Southampton county, Virginia; February 14,
         1798 . . . Norfolk (1798). 20cm. 14p.

         By David Barrow.

         STE 48359; E. Supp. B10229; NYPL 1225; Davis 138.
         Reprint William and Mary Quarterly, 1963.

98-11   A concise review of the spirit . . . late American War, com-
         pared with the spirit which now prevails; . . . (Augusta?
         1798). 12mo. 47p.

         By James Shurtleff.

         STE 34548. Cf. S. 80769, without place, and date after
         1799.

98-12   The conduct of the government of France towards the Re-
         public of Geneva . . . By a citizen of Trenton . . . Trenton

1798. 8vo. 16p.

By David Chauvet.

E. 33510; Morsch, N.J. Imprints, 379.

98-13   Defence of the alien and sedition laws . . . By Virginiensis.
Phila. . . . 1798. 8vo. 47p.

By Charles Lee.

E. 33991; S. 100583; B. Ath. p. 122; Howes L194.

98-14   The Democratic judge: or the equal liberty of the press
. . . prosecution of William Cobbett . . . By Peter Porcupine.
Philadelphia . . . 1798. 8vo. 102(2)p.; plus a variant.

By William Cobbett.

Gaines 37a,b; E. 33523; S. 13880; Pearl 31. Reprinted no.
98-60.

98-15   Democratic principles illustrated by example. By Peter Porcupine. Part the first . . . London . . . 1798. 12mo. (5)6-
23(1)p. In at least eighteen editions; plus Edinburgh,
with a variant; plus Dublin; plus Aberdeen; plus Quebec.
And see no. 98-54, Birmingham.

By William Cobbett.

Gaines 43a-g.

98-16   Democratic principles illustrated. Part the second . . . by Peter
Porcupine . . . London 1798. 12mo. (3)4-52p. In at least
twelve editions; plus Edinburgh; plus Dublin (two editions);
plus Aberdeen.

By William Cobbett.

Gaines 44a-e.

98-17   Der fortgang der menschenfresser . . . Philadelphia . . . (1798).
8vo. (3)4-32, 25-32, 41-44p.

By Anthony Aufrere. Introduction by William Cobbett.

Gaines 119; E. 33525. German edition of "The cannibals'
progress . . .".

98-18   Description of the Genesee country . . . Albany . . . 1798. 4to.,
        37p. front, 2 fold. maps, 1 fold. plan.

        By Charles Williamson.

        E. 35033; S. 104441; CHA 7916 2:5; Howes W493. (H.
        suggests also Ignatius Davis); Vail 1182.

98-19   Detection of a conspiracy, formed by the United Irishmen . . .
        subverting the government . . . by Peter Porcupine. Phila-
        delphia 1798. 8vo. (3)4-24(10)p.

        By William Cobbett.

        Gaines 38a; STE 48395; E. Supp. B10264; Pearl 34; S.
        13881 (has 1799); Dauer 150. Clark 188 doubts if by
        Cobbett.

98-20   The detection of Bache; or French diplomatic skill developed.
        (Philadelphia 1798). Broadside, 32.5x21cm.

        By William Cobbett.

        Gaines 42; E. 33524; Pearl 37; Clark 188.

98-21   Emigration to America candidly considered . . . letters . . . to his
        friend in England . . . London 1798. 8vo. viii,62p.l.

        By Thomas Clio Rickman.

        S. 71241; CHA 18731 1:6; Halk. 2p. 154. Kress S. 5563
        (that preface is by Rickman).

98-22   An enquiry whether the act of Congress . . . called the Sedition
        Bill, is unconstitutional or not. Richmond . . . 1798. Signed,
        Philodemos. 8vo. 16p.

        By William Nelson.

        Jeff. 3206; STE 34375 (supposed author). Not attr. in E.
        34375 or S. 22652.

98-23   An essay on hereditary titles, and university degrees . . . By a
        New England farmer. Boston . . . 1798. 8vo. 40p.

        By John Lowell.

E. 34022; S. 42446+. Not attr. in S. 22941.

98-24   Extract of a letter from a gentleman in America to a friend in
         England, on . . . Emigration. (London, 1798). 8vo. 29p.

         By Thomas Cooper.

         S. 16611; Bartlett 3959. Later edition of no. 94-12.

98-25   Extrait d'un ouvrage manuscrit . . . Lettres d'un Français
         voyageur . . . Philadelphia . . . (1798). 8vo. 45p.

         By Moreau de Saint-Méry.

         Monaghan 1112; Howes M788.

98-26   French arrogance . . . X. Y. Z. and the lady. Philadelphia 1798.
         8vo. (5)6-31(1)p.

         By William Cobbett.

         Gaines 40; E. 33526; S. 13883; Pearl 35; Clark p. 188.

98-27   The Gleaner. A miscellaneous production . . . By Constantia
         . . . Boston . . . 1798. 12mo., 3v, 348, 321, 328p.

         By Judith Sargent Stevens Murray.

         CHA 23125 3:7; E. 34162; S. 51531.

98-28   Guillotina, for the year 1798 . . . Hartford . . . 1798. Broad-
         side, three columns.

         By Lemuel Hopkins.

         STE 33562; NYPL 1229.

98-29   Hail Columbia. [and] A Federal ode. Boston. (1798?).
         Broadside.

         By Joseph Hopkinson.

         E. Supp. B10357; STE 48477; NYPL 1234.

98-30   The history of America, in two books . . . third edition . . .
         Philadelphia. 1798. 12mo. iv,356p.; two maps.

         By Jedidiah Morse.

E. 34147; S. 50937.

98-31   The House of wisdom in a bustle . . . noted battle lately fought
         in C-ng--ss. By Geoffrey Touchstone. Phila. . . . 1798. 8vo.
         27p. Also New York, 24p.

         By James Carey.

         Gaines 155a, b; E. 33490,92; not attr. in S. 96325 or Weg.
         608. Brin. 7031 attr. Mathew Carey.

98-32   An Impartial review of the causes and principles of the French
         Revolution. By an American. Boston . . . 1798. 8vo.
         101(1)p.

         By James Sullivan.

         E. 34620; S. 93500.

98-33   An infallible cure. For political blindness . . . (Richmond,
         1798). 16mo. 38p. Also 12mo. 24p.

         By Alexander Addison (and William Heth).

         E. 33270,71, 33873,74. S. 34690 not attr. E. 33271 says
         title and comments by Heth.

98-34   Instructions for the cavalry . . . by an officer of the militia . . .
         Albany . . . 1798. 12mo. 70,iiip.

         By David Van Horne.

         STE 34914.

98-35   Letter of a Genevan, residing at London . . . Philadelphia . . .
         1798. 8vo. 15p.

         By David Chauvet.

         E. 33511. See no. 98-12.

98-36   Letters from an American farmer . . . British colonies in North
         America . . . Philadelphia 1798. 12mo. 260p.

         By M. G. St. Jean de Crevecoeur.

         E. 33582; S. 17496. See no. 93-18.

98-37   The letters of Curtius. Addressed to . . . (John) Marshall.
         Richmond . . . 1798. 8vo. 40p.

         By John Thomson.

         E. 34657; S. 95582; Davis 406; D.A.B. 18:485. Reprinted
         over his name 1804, Shaw 7348, S. 95583 (with an introduc-
         tion probably by George Hay D.A.B. 18:484).

98-38   Letters on liberty and slavery . . . second edition . . . New York
         1798. 8vo. 24p.

         By Morgan J. Rhees.

         E. 34442; S. 70472.

98-39   The life and adventures of Peter Porcupine . . . Glasgow . . . 1798.
         12mo. (5)iv-viii(1)10-57(1)p.

         By William Cobbett.

         Gaines 19f.

98-40   The life of skunk Peter Porcupine and his two uncles. (Philadel-
         phia 1798?). 8vo. (3)4-12p.

         By James Carey.

         Gaines 156; E. 33493. S. 64164 suggests Thomas Griendlief
         "printer to the British faction in Philadelphia and New York",
         but no such printer found. See no. 98-46.

98-41   L'indépendance absolue des Américains des Etats-Unis . . . leur
         commerce . . . Paris . . . 1798. 8vo., 1p., l., 149p., l.

         By Thomas Waters Griffith.

         CHA 8535 3:5; Jeff. 3200. S. 34441 not attr.

98-42   A narrative &c. The following late transactions . . . (1798). 8vo.
         16p. Caption.

         By John Bowman.

         E. 33447.

98-43   A New scene interesting to the citizens of the United States of

America . . . by a Senator of the United States . . . (Philadelphia) 1798. 8vo. 12p.; also 8p.

By Alexander Martin.

E. 34050,51; S. 53397; Jeff. 3208; B. Ath. p. 137.

98-44   A new year's gift to the Democrats . . . third edition . . . Philadelphia . . . 1798. 8vo. (3)iv(1)6-71(1)p.

By William Cobbett.

Gaines 10h; E. 33527.

98-45   No convention. Friends, fellow-citizens and countrymen . . . by Algernon Sidney (Lexington 1798). 2p. 43.5x28.5cm.

By John Breckinridge.

Harrison p. 98. Not attr. E. Supp. B10520; STE 48615 (p. 781).

98-46   A nosegay for the young men . . . picture of the King of England, dedicated to his hireling skunk Porcupine . . . Phila. . . . (1798). 8vo. 16p.

By James Carey.

Gaines 157; E. 33494; Clark 104, 191. S. 64164 suggests Thomas Griendlief, who is named in the New York edition, "as advertised", E. 33495 (STE 33495 "a ghost"). See no. 98-40.

98-47   Observations on the emigration of Dr. Joseph Priestley . . . London . . . 1798. 8vo. 8,74,2p.; plus variant.

By William Cobbett.

Gaines 2l,m.

98-48   Observations on the Part of the United States . . . Treaty of Amity . . . (Philadelphia 1798). 4to. 17, 16p.

By John Read, Jun.

S. 68159+, 84842+. Not attr. S. 56542. This is evidently the third title to E. 34906, shown as 4to; 17,16p., and noted "signed, John Read, jun."

98-49   Observations sur tout ce qui concerne les colonies d'Amérique
        ... (n.p. 1798). 8vo. 36p.

    By G. Legal.

    S. 39848.

98-50   Oration at Rutland, Vermont, July 4, 1798 ... Rutland ... 1798.
        8vo. 31p.

    By Thomas Green Fessenden.

    E. 33733.

98-51   The original letters of Ferdinand and Elizabeth ... New York
        ... 1798. Sm. 8vo., 144p.

    By John Davis.

    CHA 5824 1:5; E. 33607. S. 57613 not attr. The author's
        journey New York to Philadelphia pp. 53-85.

98-52   The Politicians; or, a state of things ... by ... a citizen of
        Philadelphia. Phila. ... 1798. 8vo. 37(3)p.

    By John Murdock.

    Gaines 158; E. 34160; Bryan 177. Clark p. 191 attr. to
        James Murdock; S. 63819 not attr.

98-53   The President's march. A new federal song ... Philadelphia
        ... (1798). 4to. 2p.

    By Joseph Hopkinson.

    STE 33902.

98-54   Read and reflect! One pennyworth of useful wisdom ... By
        Peter Porcupine ... Birmingham (1798?). 4 leaves. Caption
        title.

    By William Cobbett.

    Gaines 43e; Pearl 38.

98-55   The recantation; being an anticipated valedictory address of

Thomas Paine.... Lexington ... 1798. 12p.

By Donald Fraser.

STE 32154; 5 Am. Imp. Inv. 73. See no. 97-52.

98-56   Reflections on Monroe's View, of the conduct of the executive
         ... under the signature of Scipio. (Philadelphia 1798). 8vo.
         88p.

         By Uriah Tracy.

         E. 34675; S. 96421; D.A.B. 18:624; Howes T326 (says this
         later than Boston ed. no. 98-62). Jeff. 3524 thought author
         Charles Lee. Ford p. vi says attr. to Alexander Hamilton
         (see S. 29982,3) erroneous. S. 62659 attr. to Timothy
         Pickering.

98-57   Remarks on the insidious letter of the gallic despots. By Peter
         Porcupine ... (Philadelphia 1798). Broadside, 43.8x26.5
         cm.

         By William Cobbett.

         Gaines 41; E. 33529; Pearl 36 semble.

98-58   Remarks on the Jacobiniad ... Part second ... Boston. 1798.
         12mo. (1)ii-xi,(2)10-56p.

         By John S. J. Gardiner.

         E. 33779; S. 26623. See no. 95-41.

98-59   A reply to an address; written by the great I ... Brimfield ...
         (Worcester) 1798. 8vo. 16p.

         By Clark Brown.

         STE 34439. Answering no. 98-03.

98-60   The Republican Judge ... partial prosecution of William Cob-
         bett ... by Peter Porcupine. London ... 1798. 8vo.
         (3)iv(1)iv, v(2)8-96(1)2p.; plus two variants; plus third edi-
         tion; plus a variant.

         By William Cobbett.

         Gaines 39a-e; S. 14013; Pearl 32. See no. 98-14.

98-61   Resolved, that the duty or trust imposed by the Constitution
         ... not ... render a Senator impeachable ... (Philadelphia,
         1798). 1 leaf. 32.5cm.

         By Jacob Read?

         E. Supp. B10487; not attr. STE 48715 (p. 875).

98-62   Scipio's reflections on Monroe's View ... Boston ... 1798.
         8vo. 2p.l., 140p.

         By Uriah Tracy.

         E. 34676; S. 96422; CHA 14732 2:3. See no. 98-56.

98-63   The second warning or strictures ... speech ... John Adams
         at the opening of Congress ... Paris. 1798. 8vo. 28p.

         By Joel Barlow?

         S. 3431, 78743; B.A.L. 895; CHA 1851 3:7. A Barlow
         biographer doubts that he wrote this. James Woodress,
         "A Yankee's Odyssey" (1958), p. 322.

98-64   Short history of the yellow fever ... Philadelphia ... second
         edition ... Philadelphia ... 1798. 8vo. 64 (i.e., 56),16p.

         By Richard Folwell.

         E. 33742; Austin 782. See no. 97-58.

98-65   The Spunkiad: or heroism improved. A congressional display
         of spit and cudgel ... By an American Youth. Newburgh
         ... 1798. 12mo. 23p.

         By John Woodworth.

         E. 35052; S. 105176+(?). In S. 89923 the attribution to
         Woodworth is said to be probably incorrect.

98-66   To the editor of Porcupine's Gazette. (n.p. 1798). 8p. caption
         title.

         By Benjamin Griffith.

         E. Supp. B10338; STE 48461.

98-67   To the Senate and Representatives of the United States ...

(caption). It is equally foreign from our wishes . . . to
criminate . . . the National Legislature . . . (Poughkeepsie
1798). Broadside, printed 2 sides.

By John Armstrong.

E. 33313. See D.A.B. 1:356; Hammond 131; Smith 393.

98-68   Truth will out! The foul charges of the Tories against the
Editor of the Aurora repelled . . . (Philadelphia 1798). 8vo.
12p.; also 2p.l.12p., two issues, with and without ornament
on p.12.

By Benjamin Franklin Bache. Also attr. William Duane.

STE 33648; CHA 23964 2:4-6; Smith p. 193-202; D.A.B.
1:463. E. 33648 and S. 20994+ (Duane); S. 97270 (either).
B.A.L. 3:255 favors Duane.

98-69   Unite or fall. Second Edition. London . . . 1798. 8vo. 23p.;
Third Edition, same, 12mo. 23p.

By Carlisle, Frederick Howard, Earl of.

S. 97838; CHA 23130 1:5.

98-70   A Versification of President Washington's . . . farewell address
. . . By a gentleman of Portsmouth, N.H. . . . Portsmouth
. . . 1798. 4to. 54p.

By Jonathan M. Sewall.

E. 34532; S. 79403; Weg. 354; D.A.B. 15:609.

98-71   What is our situation? . . . A few pages for Americans. By an
American. (Philadelphia 1798). 8vo. 40p.

By Joseph Hopkinson.

E. 33904; S. 32985, 103115+; B. Ath. p. 103; Howes H636.

1799

99-01   Address of the General Assembly to the People . . . of Virginia
         . . . Richmond. (1799).

         By James Madison.

         Malone 3:411. E. 36633; Swem 7922 not attr.

99-02   The address of the Legislature of Virginia . . . with resolutions
         . . . (Norfolk) . . . 1799. 16mo. 26p.

         By James Madison.

         Malone 3:411. E. 36634 not attr.

99-03   The address of the minority in the Virginia Legislature to the
         people of that State . . . Alien and Sedition Laws. (1799).
         8vo. 16p. Also Albany 20p.; Petersburg 16p.

         By Henry Lee.

         E. 36635-37; S. 100423; Swem 7923; B. Ath. p. 122;
         CHA 12430 3:1 (caption title). Servies 190, ascribes to John
         Marshall on the authority of Beveridge (John Marshall,
         2:402). See Malone 3:417.

99-04   An address to the freemen of Pennsylvania . . . James Ross . . .
         Germantown . . . 1799. 12mo. 24p.

         By Joseph Hopkinson.

         Cobbett pp. 60,61. E. 35081 not attr.

99-05   Address to the Republicans of Pennsylvania . . . August 7th, 1799
         . . . Philadelphia . . . 1799; also German version: An die Re-
         publicaner des Staats von Pennsylvanien . . . 1799 . . . fol. 2p.

         By Tench Coxe?

         STE 36070. E. 36070,71 not attr.

99-06   An authentic view of the progress of the State of Pennsylvania
         . . . Philadelphia, May, 1799. 8vo. 8p.

         By Tench Coxe.

E. 35361; CHA 1665 3:3. S. 59906 not attr.

99-07   The awful crisis which has arrived . . . (Richmond) 1799. fol.
        4p.

        By Henry Lee.

        E. 36638; CHA 12430 3:2. Same text as no. 99-03.

99-08   A candid examination of the objections to the treaty of amity
        . . . Great Britain . . . in Charleston . . . by a Citizen of South
        Carolina . . . Philadelphia, 1799 (1798?). 4to. 42p.

        By William Loughton Smith.

        Turnbull 372; S. 10663; E. 34907 (second title). Not STE.
        See no. 95-07.

99-09   The case of the Georgia sales on the Mississippi considered . . .
        Philadelphia . . . 1799. 4to. 91p.

        By Robert Goodloe Harper.

        E. 35587; Kress B3883. Signed on p. 44. See no. 97-13.

99-10   The Collected wisdom of ages . . . the English constitution . . .
        By Timothy Telltruth . . . Phila. . . . 1799. 8vo. 47p.

        By James Carey?

        STE 35268; not attr. STE 36401.

99-11   Consolatory odes; dedicated . . . to those unfortunate beings
        who labor under . . . the democratic mania. By Peter Quince.
        1799. 12mo.

        By Isaac Story.

        S. 92278; E. 36376, giving no paging. Question if this is
        separate. It appears in "A Parnassian Shop" (no. 01-13)
        with a title page, at p.(61), dated 1799.

99-12   The dance of Herodias, through the streets of Hartford, on
        election day . . . the strumpet of Babylon . . . 1799. 12mo.
        48p.

        By David Austin.

E. 35125; Trumb. 283; Brin. 2157; Dex. 4p.95; D.A.B. 1:432.

99-13   The Demos in council . . . pandemonium . . . Boston. April, 1799. 8vo. 16p.

By William Sullivan?

S. 93549+ ("generally attributed"). E. 35400; S. 19522 not attr.

99-14   Description of the settlement of the Genessee Country, in the State of New-York . . . letters from a gentleman . . . New-York . . . 1799. 8vo. 63p. map.

By Charles Williamson.

Vail 1221; E. 36727; S. 104442; Howes W493. See no. 98-18.

99-15   Des prisons de Philadelphie. Par un Européen . . . Amsterdam 1799. 8vo. 97p.

By La Rochefoucauld-Liancourt, Duc de.

S. 39053. See no. 96-22.

99-16   Detection of a conspiracy, formed by the United Irishmen . . . subverting the government . . . By Peter Porcupine . . . London . . . 1799. 8vo. (3)2-32p. Also Dublin 1799 (3)2-32p.

By William Cobbett.

Gaines 38b, c; Pearl 34.

99-17   The Devil let loose, or the Wo occasioned . . . discourse . . . April 25, 1799. Boston . . . 1799. 8vo. 16p.

By David Osgood.

E. 36020; S. 57771.

99-18   An elegiac poem on the death of General George Washington . . . (Philadelphia 1799). Broadside, fol.

By Charles Caldwell.

E. 36453. Query if this is a ghost of E. 37080 (1800),

no. 00-19.

99-19   An Essay on the liberty of the press . . . by Hortensius. Phila.
        . . . 1799. 12mo. (2)51p. Copyright notice inverted.

        By George Hay.

        E. 35605; S. 30997; Swem 2371; D.A.B. 8:430. Re-
        printed, with attribution to Hay, in James Lyon's "National
        Magazine" Vol. 1 Number iv, pp. 352-371 (1799). See no.
        03-10.

99-20   An estimate of commercial advantages . . . Mississippi and
        Mobile Rivers . . . Nashville . . . 1799. 8vo. 70p.

        By Zachariah Cox.

        E. 35360; A.I.I. 32:28; Howes C824. See CHA 6781 3:7.

99-21   Eumenes: . . . errors and omissions of the Constitution of New-
        Jersey . . . Trenton . . . 1799. 8vo. (1)ii-vi; (1)10-149(5)p.

        By William Griffith.

        E. 35570; S. 28829; A.I.I. 9:249; D.A.B. 7:625.

99-22   Extracts from Professor Robison's "Proofs of a conspiracy",
        . . . Boston . . . 1799, signed: Cornelius. 8vo. 30p.

        By William Bentley.

        E. 35181.

99-23   Facts and calculations . . . population and territory of the
        United States . . . (Boston 1799). 8vo. 7(1)p.

        By John Peck.

        E. 36051.

99-24   Friendly remarks . . . Connecticut . . . college and schools.
        1799. 8vo. 42p.

        By John Cosens Ogden.

        E. 36005; S. 105930; Dex. 5p. 385.

99-25   Guillotina, for the year 1799. Addressed to the readers of the
        Connecticut Courant. (Hartford 1799). Broadside, 47x28cm.

        By Lemuel Hopkins.

        E. Supp. B10754. See nos. 96-27, 96-28, 97-22, 98-28.

99-26   Letters on various interesting and important subjects . . . By
        Robert Slender, o.s.m. . . . Phila. . . . 1799. 8vo. viii(1)10-
        142p., l.

        By Philip Freneau.

        Gaines 165; E. 35516; S. 25895; Howes F377; Weg. 176;
        Leary "That Rascal Freneau" 312; Paltsits p. 77. o.s.m.
        stands for "one of the swinish multitude". B.A.L. 6450
        identifies two states, earlier has p. 47 for p. 74.

99-27   A Letter to a member of Congress; respecting the Alien and
        Sedition laws . . . Columbus, Virginia, June 6, 1799. 8vo.
        48p.

        By St. George Tucker.

        E. 36457; S. 97378; Howes T397 (with question mark).
        E. 35760 attr. James Madison. See E. 33702.

99-28   The manual of a freeman . . . political right . . . Richmond . . .
        1799. 12mo. 108(1)p.

        By Joseph Saige.

        STE 35767.

99-29   Narrative of a late expedition against the Indians . . . execution
        of Col. Crawford . . . Andover . . . (1799). 46p. Two im-
        pressions, one with "Mass." in title.

        By Hugh Henry Brackenridge.

        STE 35689, 48378; E. Supp. B10246 (1798?). CHA 5448 3:1.
        Vail 1201 not attr. E. 35689 and S. 38109 attr. to Dr. Knight.
        See no. 99-38.

99-30   Notes on the finances of the State of South-Carolina. By a
        member of the House of Representatives. Charleston . . .

(1799). 8vo. xii,32p. 3 tables.

By Henry W. Desaussure.

E. 35997; S. 87902; Turnbull p. 364; also attr. Judge William Johnson; not attr. in S. 55969.

99-31   Paine detected; or, the unreasonableness of Paine's Age of Reason. Natchez . . . 1799. (Title uncertain) (2)53p. 17.5cm.

By John Henderson.

STE 48876; E. Supp. B10807; McMurtrie 2.

99-32   Party-spirit exposed, or remarks on the times . . . By a Gentleman of New-York . . . New-York 1799. 16mo. 24p.

By Donald Fraser.

STE 35501; CHA 7559 3:6. S. 58972 semble, not attr.

99-33   Patriotic exultation on Lyon's release from the federal Bastile . . . February 12, 1799 . . . Broadside.

By Anthony Haswell.

E. 35601; Cooley 483; Spargo p. 233. McCorison 530 doubts if separate.

99-34   Plain truth: addressed to the people of Virginia. Written in February 1799 — By a Citizen of Westmoreland County . . . (1799). 16mo. 56p.

By Henry Lee.

E. 35723; S. 100508; Swem 7934; B. Ath. p. 123; Howes L203 (questions).

99-35   A poem in two cantos . . . French politics . . . By the rt. hon. Simon Spunkey, esq. . . . Vergennes or Brattleboro . . . 1799.

By Samuel Chipman, Jr?

STE 35479. Attr. to Thomas Green Fessenden E. 35479; Cooley 475; McCorison 523. No copy known. Chipman filed a copyright notice.

THE

DANCE OF HERODIAS,

Through the Streets of Hartford,

ON

ELECTION DAY,

TO THE TUNE OF

THE STARS OF HEAVEN, IN THE

DRAGON's TAIL;

O R,

A gentle trip at the heels of the Strumpet of Babylon,

Playing tricks in the attire of the

Daughters of Zion.

———

PRINTED FOR THE AUTHOR.

1799.

Attributed to David Austin. No. 99-12.

THE

Political Green-Houſe,

FOR THE YEAR 1798.

ADDRESSED TO THE READERS OF
THE CONNECTICUT COURANT,

JANUARY 1ſt, 1799.

PUBLISHED ACCORDING TO ACT OF CONGRESS.

HARTFORD:
PRINTED BY
HUDSON & GOODWIN.

Attributed to Richard Alsop, Lemuel Hopkins,
Theodore Dwight. No. 99-36.

A SHORT

HISTORY

OF LATE

Ecclefiaftical Oppreffions

IN

NEW-ENGLAND and VERMONT,

By a CITIZEN.

IN WHICH IS EXHIBITED

A STATEMENT OF THE

VIOLATION OF RELIGIOUS LIBERTIES,

WHICH ARE RATIFIED BY THE

Constitution of the United States.

RICHMOND:
PRINTED BY JAMES LYON, AT THE OFFICE OF THE NATION-
AL MAGAZINE,

1799.

Attributed to John Cosens Ogden. No. 99-41.

A

VINDICATION

O F

THOMAS JEFFERSON;

AGAINST THE CHARGES CONTAINED IN

A *PAMPHLET* ENTITLED,

" *Serious Considerations,*" *&c.*

By GROTIUS.

" O*mnes aliud agentes, aliud simulantes, perfidi,*
" *improbi, malitiosi sunt.*"   *CICERO.*

NEW-YORK,
PRINTED BY DAVID DENNISTON.

1800.

FEDERALISM TRIUMPHANT

IN THE

STEADY HABITS OF CONNECTICUT ALONE,

OR, THE

TURNPIKE ROAD TO A FORTUNE.

A COMIC OPERA OR, POLITICAL FARCE

IN SIX ACTS,

As performed at the Theatres Royal and Aristocratic at Hartford and
New-Haven October, 1801.

Ergo non satis est Risu deducere Rictum. HOR. ODE IO.
Arma, Virumque cano. VIRG.
Obscripuntque Comæ. IBID.
Is there not some chosen curse, some hidden thunder in the vaults of heaven, red with uncommon wrath, to blast the man, who owes his greatness to his country's ruin. CATO.
And the ninth vial was poured out on the great river Connecticut. REVELATIONES SECUNDUS.
But fear none of those things which thou shalt suffer, behold the devil shall cast some of you into prison, and ye shall have tribulation certain days.—But be thou faithful unto death and the reward is life. IBID.

Printed in the Year, 1802.

Attributed to Leonard Chester. No. 02-14.

AN

EXAMINATION

OF THE VARIOUS CHARGES EXHIBITED AGAINST

AARON BURR, Esq.

VICE-PRESIDENT OF THE UNITED STATES;

AND A DEVELOPEMENT

OF THE

CHARACTERS AND VIEWS

OF HIS

POLITICAL OPPONENTS.

By *ARISTIDES.*

" *I am not of the number of those men who are perpetually troubling and disturbing you ; I hold not any office of trust or of administration in the state ; I, therefore, come forward with confidence, and denounce transactions and crimes like these.*"

NEW-YORK,

PRINTED BY WARD and GOULD, opposite the CITY-HALL.

1803.

OBSERVATIONS

UPON CERTAIN PASSAGES IN

MR. JEFFERSON'S NOTES ON VIRGINIA,

WHICH APPEAR TO HAVE A TENDENCY TO

SUBVERT RELIGION,

AND ESTABLISH

A FALSE PHILOSOPHY.

NEW-YORK.

1804.

Who shall be Governor,

STRONG or SULLIVAN ?

OR THE

SHAM-PATRIOT

UNMASKED ;

BEING

AN EXPOSITION OF THE FATALLY SUCCESSFUL

ARTS OF DEMAGOGUES,

TO EXALT THEMSELVES,

BY FLATTERING AND SWINDLING

THE PEOPLE ;

IN A VARIETY OF PERTINENT FACTS,

DRAWN FROM

SACRED AND PROFANE HISTORY.

1806.

111

99-36   The political green-house, for the year 1798 . . . 1799. Hart-
         ford . . . 16mo. 24p.

         By Richard Alsop, Lemuel Hopkins, Theodore Dwight.

         E. 36133, 35634; S. 965; Weg. 745; D.A.B. 9:215.

99-37   Reflexiones sobre el comercio de Espana con sus colonias en
         America . . . Por un espanol, en Philadelphia. Philadelphia
         . . . 1799. 8vo. 90p. folded table.

         By Carlos Martinez de Yrujo, or possibly, Santiago Felipe
         Puglia.

         E. 36192 suggests Puglia. ("Perglio" is a typo.) Not attr.
         STE 36192; S. 68734. E. 38142 (no. 00-35), evidently a
         translation, is attr. to Yrujo.

99-38   A remarkable narrative of an expedition against the Indians
         . . . Col. Crawford (Leominster, Mass. 1799?). 23(1)p.

         By Hugh Henry Brackenridge.

         E. Supp. B10726; STE 48810. See no. 99-29.

99-39   Remarks on a second publication of B. Henry Latrobe, en-
         gineer . . . (Philadelphia? 1799). 8vo. 7p.

         By William Smith, provost.

         E. 36200; S. 84648; not attr. S. 60451, 62116.

99-40   Remarks on the explanation, lately published by Dr. Priestley
         . . . By Peter Porcupine. London . . . 1799. 8vo. (3)4-50,
         52(1)p.

         By William Cobbett.

         Gaines 46; S. 14012; Pearl 40; Clark p. 188.

99-41   A short history of the late ecclesiastical oppressions in New-
         England and Vermont. By a Citizen . . . Richmond . . .
         1799. 8vo. 19p.

         By John Cosens Ogden.

         E. 36006; Jeff. 3209; B. Ath. p. 153. S. 80634 not attr.

99-42   Sir, being a candidate for . . . assistant clerk to the House . . .
         Pennsylvania . . . (1799) . . . Broadside.

         By Thomas Lloyd.

         E. 36311.

99-43   The Spirit of Despotism . . . Morris-town . . . 1799. 12mo. (10)
         319p.

         By Vicesimus Knox.

         E. 35691. See no. 95-46.

99-44   A system of seamanship, and naval tactics . . . Philadelphia . . .
         1799. 8vo. 192p. 8 fold. plates.

         By John Clerk.

         E. 36393.

99-45   To the public. It is difficult to account for the rancour which
         . . . Fenno displays . . . (Philadelphia, 1799). Broadside,
         21.5cm.

         By Mathew Carey.

         Gaines 163; E. Supp. B10736; STE 48816.

99-46   To the public. The cutting a canal at Amoskeig Falls . . . (1799?)
         Broadside.

         By Samuel Blodget.

         E. Supp. B10719; STE 48805.

99-47   A View of the Calvinistic clubs in the United States. (1799?).
         16mo. 23p.

         By John Cosens Ogden.

         E. 36008; S. 99551; Brin. 2209; B. Ath. p. 152.

99-48   A View of the New England illuminati . . . destroying the
         religion and government . . . Phila. . . . 1799. 8vo. 20p.
         Also second edition, 20p.

         By John Cosens Ogden.

E. 36009, 36010; S. 99569; Jeff. 3219; B. Ath. p. 153.
See Morse 225. (E. 35269,70 attr. to James Carey).

99-49   What is our situation? and what our prospects? . . . insidious
         views of Republican France. By an American. London
         1799. 8vo. 40p.

         By Joseph Hopkinson.

         Palmer 337,8; S. 103116. Later edition of no. 98-71.

1800

00-01   Address to the citizens of Kent, on the approaching election
         . . . (Wilmington, 1800). 8vo. 14p.

         By Peregrine Letherbusy, et al.

         S. 40245. E. 36768 not attr.

00-02   Address to the citizens of South-Carolina, on the approaching
         election of President . . . By a Federal Republican. Charles-
         ton . . . 1800. 8vo. (2)34p.

         By Henry William Desaussure.

         E. 37315; S. 19682; Jeff. 3228; B.Ath. p. 244; Tompk.
         Jeff. 49; Wolfe pp. 149-151; Turnbull p. 375.

00-03   Address to the people of the United States; with an epitome
         . . . character of Thomas Jefferson. Philadelphia . . . 1800.
         Signed Americanus. 8vo. 32p.; also Newport 31p. (two
         editions, one "Second (Rhode Island) edition . . ."); Rich-
         mond 38p.

         By John James Beckley.

         E. 36917-20; S. 97904; CHA 23964; Howes B298. Not
         attr. S. 35920.

00-04   The American Rush light . . . disaffected Britons may see . . .
         perfidy of republicans . . . By Peter Porcupine . . . London

... 1800. 8vo., 2p.,l.,(1), iv-vi, (1)8-192p.; plus a variant.

By William Cobbett.

Gaines 57a, b; S. 13872; CHA 19150 2:1.

00-05   Answer to a dialogue between a Federalist and a Republican
         ... Charleston--signed, A South-Carolina Federalist ...
         1800. 8vo. 36p.

By Henry William Desaussure.

E. 37316; S. 19683; Turnbull p. 375; Beard 221n; Howes
D270. Has been ascribed to Charles Pinckney, but he was a
Republican.

00-06   An answer to Alexander Hamilton's letter concerning the pub-
         lic conduct and character of John Adams ... By a Citizen
         of New-York ... New-York ... 1800. 8vo. 32p.

By James Cheetham.

E. 37170; Ford 74; Howes C334; Wandell p. 66; Mitchell
485. Also attr. to Uzal Ogden says E.

00-07   Biographical memoirs of the illustrious Gen. Geo. Washington ...
         Phila. ... 1800. 16mo. 243p.; also 12mo. 217p.

By Thomas Condie.

E. 37222,3; S. 15176, 101779; Howes C664. Also attr. to
Thomas Childs says E. Foreword over the name of Condie.

00-08   A brief statement of opinions ... the treaty ... with Great
         Britain ... Philadelphia ... 1800. 8vo. viii,71p.

By Thomas Macdonald.

E. 37869; Gaines 169; Cobbett p. 58. E. 37428 attr. to
Thomas Fitzsimons; S. 7904 not attr.

00-09   Britain preserved. A poem in seven books. London ... 1800.
         4to. xxiv,376p.

By James Brown.

CHA 2880 2:5. S. 8064 not attr.

00-10   Bystander; or a series of letters . . . artifices of the anti-federal-
         ists . . . Baltimore . . . 1800. 12mo. 30p.

         By Robert Goodloe Harper.

         E. 37074; S. 45096; Minick 582.

00-11   The claims of Thomas Jefferson to the Presidency, examined
         at the bar of Christianity. By a layman. Philadelphia . . .
         1800. 8vo. (2)54p.

         By William Brown or Asbury Dickins.

         Brown: S. 8573; Cush. 1p. 167; NYHS 22. Dickins:
         Tompk. Jeff. 54; Dumbauld 254; Johnston, p. 27; and
         Wise & Cronin, 413. E. 37187 Brown, Dickins or Joseph
         Dennie; S. 35923 has Brown or Dickins.

00-12   The clerk's magazine; . . . forms . . . constitution . . . inhabitants
         . . . Albany . . . (1800?). 16mo. (4)310(6)p.

         By Charles R. Webster.

         STE 37192.

00-13   Communications concerning the agriculture and commerce of
         America: containing observations on the commerce of Spain
         . . . London . . . 1800. 8vo. viii,120p.

         "Observations" by Carlos Martinez de Yrujo; edited by Wil-
         liam Tatham.

         S. 106213+; Howes M352. Not attr. S. 15004. See no. 00-
         35.

00-14   The dawn of day, introductory to the rising sun . . . New-Haven
         . . . 1800. 8vo. 32p.

         By David Austin.

         E. 36867; Dexter 4p. 95; Trumb. 287.

00-15   Des prisons de Philadelphie. Par un Européen. Paris 1800. 8vo.

         By La Rochefoucauld-Liancourt, Duc de.

         S. 39053. See no. 96-22.

00-16   Desultory reflections on the new political aspects of public af-
         fairs . . . since the commencement of the year 1799 . . .
         New-York . . .1800. 8vo. 62p. Also Philadelphia 26p.

         By John Ward Fenno.

         E. 37417, 37418; Jeff. 3220; Beard p. 221. S. 19584 attr.
         to James [sic] Dennie; S. 19771, not attr. B.A.L. vol. 2,
         p. 441, doubts attr. to Joseph Dennie. S. 19771 notes a
         second part of 38 pages (see next item). For description,
         see Dauer p. 193-5.

00-17   Desultory reflections on the political aspects of public affairs
         in the United States of America. Part II . . . New-York . . .
         1800. 8vo. (2)38p.

         By John Ward Fenno.

         E. 37419; S. 24074. See B.A.L. vol. 2, p. 441, and preced-
         ing item.

00-18   A dirge . . . commemorating . . . George Washington . . .
         (Boston 1800). 8vo. 4p.

         By John M. Williams.

         E. 39106; S. 104278; not attr. S. 51578.

00-19   An elegiac poem on the death of General George Washington
         . . . (Philadelphia) 1800. Broadside (two editions).

         By Charles Caldwell.

         E. 37079-80; Stillwell 301. Reprinted over his name in
         same year E. 37077; Stillwell 47. See next entry.

00-20   An elegiac poem on the death of George Washington . . .
         Springfield . . . 1800. 12mo. 11p.

         By Charles Caldwell.

         E. 37078. See preceding entry.

00-21   Epistle from the Marquis de la Fayette, to General Washington
         . . . Edinburgh . . . 1800. 12mo., 2p., l., 32p. In verse.

         By George Hamilton?

CHA 8856 2:6, supposed author; S. 30010. Not attr. S. 38570; Edinburgh 2:714. S. 101802 also suggests Anne Bannerman and Hugh Hamilton.

00-22 Epistle to Peter Pindar . . . trial . . . for publishing a libel on Anthony Pasquin . . . New York . . . 1800. (2)128, xip. 2pl?

By William Gifford.

STE 37514. (Anthony Pasquin is J. M. Williams; see no. 04-26.)

00-23 An epitome of the life & character of Thomas Jefferson. (Wilmington 1800). 8vo. 8p.

By John James Beckley.

E. 36921; Wise & Cronin 323; S. 97904. Reprinted from no. 00-03.

00-24 Essay on political society . . . Philadelphia, 1800. 8vo. (7)10-234p.

By Samuel W. Dana?

E. 37381. S. 22947 not attr.

00-25 Eulogy on George Washington . . . Georgetown, S.C. . . . 1800. 8vo. 19p.

By Francis Kinloch.

E. 37735; S. 37922.

00-26 A few remarks on Mr. Hamilton's late letter, concerning the public conduct & character, of the President. By Caius . . . Balt. . . . 1800. 8vo. 24p.

By William Pinkney.

E. 38271; Ford 75; Jeff. 3238; Minick 619. See Smith, P., 2:1045; not attr. S. 9863.

00-27 Funeral oration. (Philadelphia, 1800). 8vo. 17p.

By Henry Lee.

E. 37797; S. 39744; Stillwell 131.

00-28   The honourable Mr. Sedgwicks' political last will and testament
         ... (Stockbridge?) ... 1800. 8vo. 21p.

         By Barnabas Bidwell?

         Authorship attr. in Boston Public Library copy. See Richard
         E. Welch, Jr. "Theodore Sedgwick, Federalist", p. 233 note;
         E. 37645 not attr.

00-29   Hymns composed on the death of Gen. Washington ... Ports-
         mouth ... 1800. 8vo. 4p.

         By George Richards.

         E. 38400; S. 70920.

00-30   An impartial review of the rise and progress of the controversy
         between ... Federalists & Republicans ... Phila. ... 1800.
         8vo. 50p.

         By Charles Pettit.

         E. 38239; CHA 5981 1:5; Howes I15. S. 34383 not attr.

00-31   An investigation of that false, fabulous and blasphemous mis-
         representation ... By Thomas Paine ... By a Delaware Wag-
         goner (1800). 12mo. 192p.

         By D. Nelson.

         STE 38028; S. 34960 (with "?").

00-32   A letter to General Hamilton, occasioned by his letter to Presi-
         dent Adams. By a Federalist. Signed, Aristides. (New York?
         1800). 8vo. 8p. (four editions); (3)4-10p.; 15p.

         By Noah Webster, Jr.

         E. 39045-7; S. 102361; Skeel 727-732; Gaines 170. Ford 77
         has "Alexander" Hamilton. Tapley 371 is Salem edition 32p.,
         attr. to James Cheetham, E. 39048 says "ghost".

00-33   A Letter to Major General Alexander Hamilton containing observa-
         tions on his letter concerning ... John Adams ... By a Citizen

of These States. New York . . . 1800. 8vo. 32p.; also Salem
28(1)p.

By Uzal Ogden.

E. 38152,3; Ford 79; Brin. 4952; Howes H118. Tapley
373 is Salem edition.

00-34   Minutes of Debates in Council, on the banks of the Ottawa
         River . . . Indian nations, who defeated the Army of the
         United States . . . Baltimore . . . 1800. 8vo. 23p.

         By Alexander McKee?

         See "The Month at Goodspeed's", Vol. 34 at p. 215. Not
         attr. in E. 37968; S. 49351. See no. 92-19.

00-35   Observations on the commerce of Spain with her colonies in
         time of war . . . By a Spaniard, in Philadelphia . . . Phila-
         delphia . . . 1800. 8vo. vii(5)10-63p. tab.

         By Carlos Martinez de Yrujo.

         E. 38142; S. 106218. See no. 99-37.

00-36   Observations on the proposed state road, from Hudson's
         River . . . to Lake Erie . . . New-York . . . 1800. 8vo. 18p.
         folded map.

         By Charles Williamson.

         Vail 1265; E. 39109; S. 104444.

00-37   An ode in honor of the Pennsylvania militia . . . George Wash-
         ington . . . Albany 1800. 12mo. 10p.

         By Hugh Henry Brackenridge.

         E. 37031; S. 101861+; Weg. 874. Not attr. S. 56702. First
         published 1777, S. 7185.

00-38   An oration, "On the extent and power of political delusion",
         has lately been reprinted . . . the public are in turn presented
         with A rod for the fool's back . . . Bennington . . . (1800?).
         16mo. 15p.

         By Noah Webster, Jr.

E. 39049; S. 102396+; Skeel 726; McCorison 589. S. 5598 not attr. See no. 00-43.

00-39   A poem on the President's farewell address. With a sketch of the character of his successor. Second edition. Philadelphia . . . (1800?). 8vo. 8p.

By St. John Honeywood.

E. 37644. However, see no. 97-40.

00-40   The Prospect before us. Volume I (Vol. II, Part I). Richmond . . . 1800. 12mo. 184p. (and 8vo. 152p.).

By James Thomson Callender.

E. 37083,4; S. 10068; Tompk. Jeff. 24; Howes C72; Jeff. 3518; D.A.B. 3:425. See no. 01-16 for later part.

00-41   Reflections on Crimes and Punishments. [caption title] 12p. (1800+?).

By Samuel Austin.

McCorison 2249.

00-42   Report of the Committee . . . proceedings of sundry of the other states in answer to the resolutions of the General Assembly . . . Richmond (1800). 12mo. 71p. Also Raleigh, N.C., 1800.

By James Madison.

Cronin & Wise, Madison 89; Brant 1787-1800, p. 467; Malone 3:422. Not attr. in E. 38961; or Swem 7972.

00-43   A rod for the fool's back . . . (New Haven? 1800). 8vo. 10p.; 11p.; 12p.

By Noah Webster, Jr.

E. 39052-4; S. 102396; Trumb. 1601, 2819 (10p.); Skeel 723-25.

00-44   The Rush-Light. 15th Feb. 1800 . . . By Peter Porcupine. New York. 8vo. (2)1-46p.; plus edition with "New Yokk"; plus edition with "Ruhsite" p. 41.

By William Cobbett.

Gaines 51a-c.

00-45   The Rush-Light. 28th Feb. 1800 . . . By Peter Porcupine . . .
         New York. 8vo. (2)47-112p.; plus another edition; plus
         three variants.

         By William Cobbett.

         Gaines 52a-e.

00-46   The Rush-Light. 15th March, 1800 (New York 1800). 8vo.
         113-160(4)p.; plus three variants.

         By William Cobbett.

         Gaines 53a-d.

00-47   The Rush-Light. 31st March, 1800 (New York 1800). 8vo.
         161-208p.; plus two variants.

         By William Cobbett.

         Gaines 54a-c.

00-48   The Rush-Light. 30th April, 1800. (New York 1800). 8vo.
         209-258(2)p.

         By William Cobbett.

         Gaines 55.

00-49   The Rush-Light. 30th August, 1800 (London 1800). 8vo.
         (1)260-309(1)p.; plus same (New York? 1800).

         By William Cobbett.

         Gaines 56a, b.

00-50   Sacred dirges . . . death of General George Washington . . . an
         original composition. By a citizen of Massachusetts . . .
         Boston . . . (1800). 8vo. 24p. Also second issue, 8vo. 24,
         4p. Issues priced 50 cents and 37½ cents.

         By Oliver Holden.

CHA 7820 3:7, 3:5; E. 37635; S. 32475, 101879+.

00-51 Serious Considerations on the Election of a President . . . New-
       York . . . 1800. 8vo. 36p.; also Trenton . . . 1800. 8vo.
       31p.

       By William Linn.

       E. 37835,36; S. 41347; Howes L365. Jeff. 3226 is Trenton
       ed. Tompk. Jeff. 201. See no. 00-63. STE 37836 has 24p.;
       S. 41347 says assisted by John M. Mason.

00-52 Serious facts opposed to "Serious Considerations:" . . . Warning
       to religious Republicans . . . October, 1800. Signed, Marcus
       Brutus. 8vo. 16p.

       By Benjamin Pollard?

       E. 38486; Cush. 2 p. 21. S. 35932, 79263 not attr.

00-53 Sketch of a discourse . . . late General George Washington . . .
       Dublin . . . 1800. 8vo. (4)20p.

       By Matthew Carr.

       CHA 3899 2:1; S. 101884; Stillwell 49, 304.

00-54 A solemn address . . . approaching election of a president of the
       United States . . . New-York . . . 1800. Signed, Timoleon.
       8vo. 36p.

       By Tunis Wortman.

       E. 39149; S. 105513; Tompk. Jeff. 280; CHA 11471 1:6.

00-55 A statement of the measures contemplated against Samuel
       Bryan . . . register general . . . Pennsylvania . . . Phila. . . .
       1800. 8vo. 62p.

       By Samuel Bryan?

       LCP 882; S. 8800. Not attr. in E. 38557; S. 60642, 90746.

00-56 Strictures upon the letter imputed to Mr. Jefferson, addressed
       to Mr. Mazzei. Printed, June, 1800. Signed "Greene". 8vo.
       12p.

By Tench Coxe.

E. 37265; S. 92859+. Not attr. in Tompk. Jeff. 258; S. 35933.

00-57 A system of exchange with almost all parts of the world . . . New York . . . 1800. 12mo. iv(1)14-180p.

By Joseph James and Daniel Moore.

E. 37696; Kress B4207 (has James only).

00-58 Three letters to Abraham Bishop . . . his oration . . . September 1800 . . . By Connecticutensis. Hartford . . . 1800. 8vo. 36p.; Bennington 8vo. 36p.

By David Daggett.

E. 37281,82; S. 95742; Dex. 4p. 263. See Fisher p. 99. Also attr. to Elizur Goodrich. Skeel p. 563 no. 6 says attribution to Noah Webster is erroneous. S. 5591, 15875 no attribution. Bennington edition, McCorison 563. S. 105939 has a New Haven edition, not described, from E. 37283.

00-59 To the freemen of Rhode-Island, &c . . . signed, A Republican. (Providence 1800). 8vo. 16p.

By Jonathan Russell.

E. 38438; S. 74357; Tompk. Jeff. 243; Alden 1704.

00-60 A tribute to Washington, for February 22d, 1800 . . . Troy . . . 1800. 8vo. 15p.

By John Lovett.

E. 37852; S. 42387; Weg. 1049.

00-61 A vindication of the general ticket law . . . Virginia . . . Richmond . . . 1800. 8vo. 23(1)7p.

By George Hay?

E. 38943. Not attr. S. 99807; Swem 7962; STE 38943.

00-62 A vindication of the religion of Mr. Jefferson . . . by a friend to real religion . . . Baltimore . . . (1800). 8vo. 21p.

By Samuel Knox.

E. 37702; S. 99824+; Jeff. v:191; Wise & Cronin 547;
D.A.B. 10:481. S. 35936 not attr.

00-63   A vindication of Thomas Jefferson; against the charges contained in a pamphlet entitled, "Serious considerations,"
&c. By Grotius . . . New-York . . . 1800. 8vo. 47p.

By DeWitt Clinton.

E. 37195; S. 13724; Jeff. 3197; D.A.B. 4:222. See
no. 00-51.

00-64   The voice of warning, to christians, on the ensuing election of
a president of the United States . . . New-York . . . 1800.
8vo. 40p.

By John Mitchell Mason.

E. 37904; S. 45463; Tompk. Jeff. 216; Wise & Cronin
595.

00-65   The Wilmingtoniad, or a touch at the times. A dialogue . . .
Wilmington . . . 1800. 16mo. 19p.

By John Vaughan?

Jeff. 3274 suggests Vaughan; E. 39115 suggests Vaughan
or the printer, James Wilson; S. 104590 not attr.; Reed
2606 has Joseph Bringhurst.

1801

01-01   An account of the state prison . . . in the City of New York
. . . 1801. 8vo. 94, 83-97(1)p., incl. 2 fold. tab.; plus 2
engraved plans.

By Thomas Eddy.

S. 21816; Shaw 431; Jeff. 2365; D.A.B. 6:15. See NYHS
Quarterly, April 1963, p. 143.

01-02   An address to the electors of the State of New York. Albany
         ... (1801). 16mo. 34p. Also New York 1801. 12mo.
         23p.

         By Alexander Hamilton.

         S. 29947; Ford 83; Shaw 605, 606. See Wise & Cronin
         488.

01-03   Address to the well-disposed ... Westchester County ... ensu-
         ing election ... New-York ... 1801. 8vo. 32p.

         By Samuel Bayard.

         Jeff. 3266; Shaw 21 as corrected; S. 4039.

01-04   Biographical memoirs of General George Washington ... Third
         edition ... Phila. 1801. 24mo. 217p.

         By Thomas Condie.

         S. 15177; Shaw 337. See no. 00-07.

01-05   Considerations on the government of the Territory of Columbia:
         ... under the signature of Epaminondas. Washington ...
         1801. 8vo. 18p.

         By Augustus B. Woodward.

         S. 105149; Jeff. 3256; Swem 6667; Cush. 1p. 92; D.A.B.
         20:506. See no. 01-08.

01-06   The Delawariad, or a second part of the Wilmingtoniad ... A
         dialogue ... Wilmington ... 1801. 8vo. 16p. (Shaw has
         22p.).

         By Joseph Bringhurst?

         Reed 2606. Shaw 402 not attr. See no. 00-65.

01-07   A Dissertation upon the constitutional freedom of the press ...
         By an Impartial Citizen ... Boston ... 1801. 8vo. 54p.

         By James Sullivan.

         S. 93496; 40 A.I.I. 272; D.A.B. 18:191.

01-08   Epaminondas on the government of the Territory of Columbia,

No. V. George-Town, Territory of Columbia . . . 1801. 8vo. 13p.

By Augustus B. Woodward.

S. 105152; Tompk. Jeff. 61; Jeff. 3257, 3465. See no. 01-05.

01-09   An examination of the President's reply to the New-Haven remonstrance . . . list of removals from office . . . New-York . . . 1801. By Lucius Junius Brutus. 8vo. 69p. 1l.

By William Cranch (or possibly William Coleman).

Skeel p. 523 no. 4: Noah Webster's copy has his note ascribing it to William Cranch, a brother-in-law of his wife. Attr. to Cranch in Purcell p. 426; Cush. 1 p. 42. Attr. to Coleman: S. 14312, 23365; Howes C573; Tompk. Jeff. 33. In Johnston, Coleman is given on p. 17 and Cranch suggested on p. 29.

01-10   Jefferson and liberty . . . a patriotic tragedy . . . by Nichols . . . (Boston) 1801. 8vo. 28p.

By J. Horatio Nichols.

Shaw 1054. Johnston 29; Wise & Cronin 614 have William Nichols; S. 55187 does not give first name.

01-11   Knoxville, September 24th, 1801. Dear Sir . . . 2p.

By Andrew Jackson.

Shaw 704.

01-12   Letter to a member of the General Assembly of Virginia . . . conspiracy of the slaves . . . Baltimore . . . 1801. 8vo. 23p. Also Richmond, 8vo. 21p. 2d ed. 21p.

By George Tucker.

McLean 52, 180, 241; Davis p. 420. Attr. to St. George Tucker in S. 97378+, 100484; Bristol 37; not attr. in S. 40410.

01-13   A Parnassian Shop . . . By Peter Quince, Esq. Boston. 1801. 12mo. 155p.

By Isaac Story.

S. 92282; Cush. 1 p. 244; Shaw 1367; D.A.B. 18:102.
Halk. 4 p. 303 is Philadelphia edition?

01-14   Poems chiefly in the Scottish dialect . . . by a native of Scotland . . . Washington (Pa.) . . . 1801. 12mo. xii, 126p.
7 leaves.

By David Bruce.

Shaw 244; Gaines 172; S. 8730; Weg. 888.

01-15   Political intolerance, or the violence of party spirit; exempli-
fied in a recent removal from office . . . By one of the
American People . . . Boston . . . 1801. 8vo. 36p.

By Winthrop Sargent.

S. 77040; Brin. 4917; Johnston 30; Wise & Cronin 635.

01-16   The Prospect before us. Vol. II, pt. 2. Richmond . . . 1801.
8vo. 96p.

By James Thomson Callender.

S. 10068; Howes C72; Tompk. Jeff. 25; CHA 3408 2:3.
See no. 00-40.

01-17   Remonstrance of the merchants of New-Haven on the appoint-
ment of Samuel Bishop, Esq. Collector . . . (1801). No
copy found.

By Noah Webster and Simeon Baldwin?

Skeel p. 522 no. 4 attr. to Webster. Baldwin p. 295 attr. to
Baldwin. A reply to the Remonstrance by Abraham Bishop,
son of Samuel, in the Sun of Liberty, Sept. 9, 1801, reprinted in "Public documents . . . New Haven Remonstrance
. . ." (London 1814) states (third par.) that the Remonstrance
was written by "two federal lawyers". This would fit Baldwin. It would also fit Webster, except that he had abandoned
practice in 1793. Bishop suggests (final par.) that Webster be
hired to produce "another rod for the fool's back" (see no.
00-43) in reply, possibly indicating that Webster was not the
author of the Remonstrance.

01-18   A reply to Lucius Junius Brutus's Examination of the President's Answer . . . By Leonidas. New York . . . 1801. 8vo. 62(3)p.

By James Cheetham?

DuPuy 1417: "Probably this was written by James Cheetham". It was printed by his firm. Not attr. in Jeff. 3271; S. 40117; Shaw 815.

01-19   The Spirit of the Farmer's Museum and Lay Preacher's Gazette. Being a judicious selection . . . Walpole . . . 1801. 12mo. 318, (3)p.

By Joseph Dennie, Royall Tyler (as Spondee), et al.

S. 89498; B.A.L. 4636; D.A.B. 19:97. See Mott p. 255, et. seq.

01-20   Strictures on a pamphlet entitled "An examination of the President's reply to the New-Haven remonstrance . . . By Tullius Americus . . . Albany . . . 1801. 8vo. 38p.

By Abraham Bishop?

S. 97440; Tompk. Jeff. 259; Howes B473. Not Dexter; not attr. Shaw 60.

01-21   A Supplement to the fourth part of Dr. Priestley's Lectures on History . . . New Haven . . . 1801. 8vo. 14p.

By Ebenezer Grant Marsh.

Dex. 5 p. 155; S. 93804; Shaw 869.

01-22   Thoughts on the increasing wealth and national economy of the United States . . . Washington . . . 1801. 8vo. 40p. table. Preface signed Observator.

By Samuel Blodget, Jr.

S. 5958, 95708; Jeff. 3254; Howes B538; D.A.B. 2:381.

01-23   To the electors of New-Castle County, Wilmington, Del. (1801). 12p.

By Charles Anderson.

Shaw 65; Reed 2607.

01-24   To the public . . . Constitution of the Washington Printing and
        Bookselling Co. . . . [Washington, D.C., 1801]. Broadside.

        By James Lyon.

        Cunningham 242; not attr. in Shaw 1611.

01-25   The Trial of Republicanism: or, a series of political papers . . .
        By Peter Porcupine . . . London . . . 1801. 8vo. (3)4-63(1)p.

        By William Cobbett.

        Gaines 47; S. 64166, 96805+; Howes C524; Pearl 42.

01-26   Voyage dans la haute Pensylvanie et dans l'état de New-York
        . . . Paris . . . 1801. 3v., maps, plates, ports., some on large
        paper.

        By Michel Guillaume Jean de Crèvecoeur.

        CHA 5465 3:5; S. 17501. German edition 1802; S. 69136.

1802

02-01   The address of the state committee of Republicans . . . of Penn-
        sylvania . . . election of 1802. Philadelphia . . . 1802. 8vo.
        16p.

        By Alexander James Dallas.

        Higginbotham p. 46. Shaw 2134 not attr.

02-02   An Address to the people of the United States on the policy
        of maintaining a permanent navy. By an American Citizen.
        Phila. . . . 1802. 8vo. iv(1)6-51p.

        By Enos Bronson?

        S. 97903; CHA 2918 1:1; Howes B803; also attr. to Albert
        Gallatin.

02-03   Address to the people of the United States . . . epitome and vindication ... Thomas Jefferson. By Americanus. Phila. 1802; Worcester 1802 ... 8vo. 32p.

By John James Beckley.

S. 97904; Howes B298; Nichols 427, 1349. See no. 00-03. Not attr. S. 35920.

02-04   Annals of the corporation, relative to the late contested elections ... by Lysander ... New-York ... 1802. 8vo. 90p.

By James Cheetham.

S. 12373, 42881; Jeff. 3325.

02-05   An Antidote to John Wood's poison. By Warren. New York ... 1802 ... 8vo. 63p.

By James Cheetham.

S. 12374; Tompk. Burr 23; Brin. 4796; Wandell p. 64.

02-06   Authentic information relative to the conduct of the President ... Wilmington ... 1802. Signed, A friend to liberty. 12mo. 32p.

By Theodorus Bailey.

Johnston 30; Wise & Cronin 306. Shaw 1792 not attr.

02-07   Church and State, a political union, formed by the enemies of both ... 1802. 8vo. iv, 60p.

By Abraham Bishop.

S. 5592; Dex. 4:22; Morse 225.

02-08   Conciliation. An Oration ... Shoreham, July 5, 1802. Middlebury ... 1802. 8vo. 20p.

By Timothy Page.

McCorison 652; Shaw 2835.

02-09   The crisis of the sugar colonies ... effects of the French expedition to the West Indies ... London ... 1802. 8vo. vii,222p.

By James Stephen.

CHA 20772 1:2; S. 17530, 91235+, 102829+.

02-10 A description of the eastern coast of the county of Barnstable
       . . . Boston . . . 1802. 8vo. 15p.

       By James Freeman?

       Shaw 2255.

02-11 Essex Junto; or quixotic guardian. A comedy . . . By a citizen
       of Massachusetts . . . Salem 1802. 12mo. 71p.

       By J. Horatio Nichols.

       Tapley p. 384; Shaw 2795. S. 23019 not attr.

02-12 The Examination of the President's Message, at the opening of
       Congress December 7, 1801 . . . New-York . . . 1802. Signed,
       Lucius Crassus. 8vo. 127p.

       By Alexander Hamilton.

       S. 29953; Ford 86; Tompk. Jeff. 80; Shaw 2363; not attr.
       S. 17426.

02-13 A farmer's letters to the people. Phila. . . . 1802. 8vo. 95p.

       By Levi Lincoln.

       S. 41255; Tompk. Jeff. 200; Howes L345; Wise & Cronin
       564. See no. 02-20.

02-14 Federalism triumphant in the steady habits of Connecticut
       alone . . . 1802. 8vo. iii(1)5-40p.

       By Leonard Chester.

       Howard p. 203; Hill 41; CHA 4294 1:1; Shaw 2026. S.
       15737 not attr.

02-15 A friend to the Constitution. (n.p. 1802). 8vo. 60p.

       By Daniel Carroll?

       DuPuy 625. So endorsed in later hand on compiler's copy.
       In opposition to repeal of the Judiciary Act, which Congress
       effected March 3, 1802. Not attr. S. 25946; Shaw 538.

02-16 Hints toward promoting the health and cleanliness of the City of New York. New York . . . 1802. 16p. plate.

By William Sabatier?

Austin 1698.

02-17 The historic progress . . . liberty . . . over faction . . . By a farmer . . . Portsmouth 1802. 8vo. 54p., errata slip.

By Oliver Whipple.

S. 103309; Shaw 3549; NYHS 118.

02-18 Letters of Shahcoolen, a Hindu Philosopher, residing in Philadelphia . . . 1802. 12mo. 152p.

By Benjamin Silliman.

See introduction by Ben H. McClary to 1962 edition, Scholar's Facsimiles & Reprints, Gainesville, Fla. Attr. to Samuel L. Knapp in S. 38076, 79687; Shaw 2490.

02-19 Letters to Alexander Hamilton, King of the Feds . . . By Tom Callender, Esq. . . . New-York . . . 1802. 8vo. 64p.

By James Thomson Callender?

S. 10065; Howes C70; Johnston 30; CHA 3408 1:7. However, Ford 88 notes that the work attacks Callender. Shaw 1984 not attr. I think it is not by Callender.

02-20 Letters to the people. By a Farmer . . . Salem . . . 1802. 12mo. 102p.

By Levi Lincoln.

S. 41256; Tompk. Jeff. 200; Jeff. 3442; Tapley p. 384; D.A.B. 11:263. See no. 02-13.

02-21 A letter to Thomas Jefferson, President . . . by Junius Philaenus. New-York . . . 1802. 8vo. 64p.

By Paul R. Johnson?

Johnston 31; Howes J77 (probably); CHA 17497 1:7. Shaw 2525; S. 36926 not attr. Johnson was the printer.

02-22   A mirror exhibited, by the sayings . . . greatest men in Europe
         . . . Boston . . . 1802. 55p.

         By Daniel Humphreys.

         Shaw 2668, corrected.

02-23   A narrative of the suppression by Col. Burr of the History of
         the Administration of John Adams . . . By a citizen of New-
         York. New York . . . 1802. 8vo. 72p.; plus second edition,
         same; plus Baltimore 72p.

         By James Cheetham.

         S. 12380; Tompk. Burr 21; Cronin & Wise, Adams 126;
         Wandell p. 60; D.A.B. 4:47; CHA 3147 1:3-6, 4278 1:2.

02-24   A narrative, or journal of voyages and travels, through the North-
         west continent of America . . . 1789 and 1793 . . . London
         . . . 1802. 8vo., 2p., l., 91p.

         By Sir Alexander Mackenzie.

         CHA 13230 1:7.

02-25   A new arrangement of the Courts of Justice . . . Maryland:
         proposed . . . Maryland . . . 1802. 8vo. 66p.

         By John Leeds Bozman.

         S. 45268; Bristol 91; Shaw 1942.

02-26   Requisites for, and complete method of hog-teaching. Phila.
         . . . (1802). 8vo. 11p.

         By Michael Leib?

         Shaw 9247 as corrected by PPL.

02-27   Selections from . . . Abbé Baruel's "Memoirs . . ." Pittsfield.
         1802. 8vo. 23p.

         By William Bentley?

         The author notes (p. 3) he wrote no. 99-22, attr. to Bentley.
         Not attr. Shaw 1844.

02-28   A series of letters, addressed to Thomas Jefferson . . . his of-
         ficial conduct and principles . . . By Tacitus. Philadelphia
         . . . 1802. 8vo. 127, (45), (2)p.

         By Thomas Evans.

         S. 23186, 94189; B. Ath. 246; Howes E229; Tompk. Jeff.
         63; Shaw 2198.

02-29   The Sham-Patriot unmasked . . . arts of demagogues . . . by
         Historicus- -Hudson . . . 1802. 12mo. 143p. (two issues);
         also Middletown (Conn.) 16mo. 92p.

         By Ezra Sampson.

         S. 75929, 79740; Dex. 3 p. 504; Brin. 4919; Shaw 3045-
         47.

02-30   A specimen of Republican institutions . . . Philadelphia . . .
         1802. 16mo. 81p.

         By Samuel W. Dana?

         S. 89123. Shaw 2115, cancelled; Shaw 3106 not attr.

02-31   The standard of liberty. An occasional paper. By Democritus.
         (Philadelphia 1802). 8vo. 55p.; also 80p.

         By Hugh Henry Brackenridge.

         S. 7192; Cush. 1 p. 79; B.A.L. 1308 (80p.); Shaw 1943,44.

02-32   Thoughts on the subject of a health establishment for the city
         of Philadelphia. (Phila. 1802). 16p.

         By Charles Caldwell.

         Austin 396; not attr. in Shaw 3164.

02-33   A View of the political conduct of Aaron Burr, Esq. Vice Presi-
         dent . . . New-York . . . 1802. 8vo. 120p.

         By James Cheetham.

         S. 12387; Tompk. Burr 22; Howes C340; Jeff. 3443; Wan-
         dell p. 64; D.A.B. 4:47. See Hammond 124, 136, 141, 188.
         CHA 3147 2:2,3 notes four issues with textual and typo-

graphical variations, giving one example: line 10-11 of title ... Cheetham//No. 142 ... or else ... Pearl//Street ...

02-34   Voyage à la Louisiane ... dans les années 1794 à 1798 ... Par B__ D___ ... Paris ... 1802. viii, 382p. map.

By Louis Narcisse Baudry des Lozières.

Clark, ed., II:76; S. 3979, 100802+; Howes B243; Monaghan 149; CHA 12987 1:2.

1803

03-01   An account of Louisiana ... abstract of documents ... Philadelphia ... 1803. 8vo. 50p., fold. tab. Also Albany, 48p., Carlisle 21p., Philadelphia 48p., Providence 72p., (Washington) 48p., (Raleigh) 28p., Wilmington 76p. Some with appendix (2)xcp.

By Jacob Wagner.

Malone, vol. 4, p. 340. B.A.L. 1507; Howes L493 suggest John Sibley. See Jeff. 3166a (vol. v p. 207); CHA 12979; Shaw 3615-22, 5196-9. S. 42177 not attr. Wagner was chief clerk in the State Department.

03-02   An account of the proceedings of the Illinois and Oubache Land Companies ... Philadelphia ... 1803. 8vo. 14, 74p.

By William Smith, provost.

S. 84578; CHA 20127 1:3. Later edition of no. 96-02.

03-03   An address on the past, present, and eventual relations of the United States to France. New-York ... 1803. By Anticipation. 8vo. 20p.

By John Dickinson.

S. 20042; Jeff. 3299; Shaw 4081; NYHS 112; not attr. in S. 405.

03-04   An Address to the citizens of Connecticut. Signed, Chatham.
         (1803). 8vo. 24p.

         By Noah Webster, Jr.

         S. 102333; Shaw 5554; Dex. 4 p. 74; Skeel 734. S. 15640
         not attr.

03-05   An address to the freemen of Connecticut . . . Hartford . . .
         1803. 8vo. 7p.

         By Noah Webster, Jr.

         S. 102333+; Skeel p. 523, no. 6; not attr. in S. 15644;
         Shaw 3636, 4189.

03-06   An address to the government of the United States, on the
         cession of Louisiana to the French . . . Philadelphia . . .
         1803. 8vo. (2)92p.; also 56p.

         By Charles Brockden Brown.

         S. 8457, 42188; B.A.L. 1504, 1505; Howes B831; Streeter
         1574.

03-07   A brief statement of the origin and progress of the Connecticut
         intrusion in the State of Pennsylvania. (Philadelphia 1803).
         9p.

         By William Tilghman.

         Shaw 50395 (addenda).

03-08   A defence against calumny, or . . . Christopher Ellery . . . hung
         . . . (Newport). 1803. 8vo. 64p. Also New York?

         By John Rutledge.

         S. 74487; Shaw 5008. Shaw 4053,54 not attr.

03-09   An epitome of Mr. Forsyth's treatise . . . fruit-trees . . . By an
         American farmer. Philadelphia . . . 1803. 8vo. (5)2-186(6)p.;
         fifteen plates.

         By William Cobbett.

         Gaines 63a; Pearl 54; S. 25154.

03-10   An essay on the liberty of the Press. Respectfully inscribed to
         the Republican printers . . . By Hortensius . . . Richmond
         . . . 1803. 30, 48p.

         By George Hay.

         Jeff. 2022. In two parts. The first part is reprint of no. 99-
         19. Shaw 4353 and 4354 list as separate pamphlets. See
         Leonard W. Levy, Legacy of Suppression (Harvard, 1960),
         p. 269. S. 30997.

03-11   An essay, on the means of improving public education adapted
         to the United States . . . Fredericktown . . . 1803. (2), 14p.

         By Samuel Knox.

         Bristol 196; Shaw 4487; D.A.B. 10:481.

03-12   An examination of the question who is the writer of two forged
         letters addressed to the President . . . Washington City . . .
         1803. 8vo. 24p. Also second edition, n.p., 8vo. 21p.

         By William Duane.

         S. 20985, 74488; Turnbull p. 400; Shaw 4109-4111; Jeff.
         3300 lists under John Rutledge (see Wolfe pp. 179-181).

03-13   An Examination of the various charges exhibited against Aaron
         Burr, Esq. . . . views of his political opponents. By Aristides
         . . . New-York . . . 1803. 8vo. (4)l.5-118p.l. Also Philadel-
         phia 77p. (two issues: page 4 in one begins "Ready"; in the
         other "terest").

         By William Peter Van Ness.

         S. 98529; Tompk. Burr 103; Jeff. 3446; Howes V37;
         Wandell p. 12; D.A.B. 19:202; CHA 4278 3:4. Answer to
         no. 02-33. See Hammond 141, 188.

03-14   Facts are stubborn things or nine plain questions to the people
         of Connecticut . . . By Simon Holdfast . . . Hartford . . .
         1803. 8vo. 23p.

         By David Daggett.

         Dex. 4 p. 263; Purcell p. 426; not attr. S. 32482.

03-15   Gleanings . . . on husbandry . . . observations by a gentleman of
         Philadelphia. Philadelphia . . . 1803. viii, 365p., plate.

         "Observations" by John Beale Bordley?

         Kress B4631, attr. in ms. on MH. copy; Shaw 4284 not attr.

03-16   Interesting account of the project of France respecting Louisiana
         . . . Martinsburg (W.Va.) . . . 1803. 16mo. (2)48p.

         By William Coleman and Charles Brockden Brown?

         B.A.L. 1:308 quotes from the wrapper: "The following is a
         review (by the editor of the New-York Herald) of a pamphlet
         . . . (no. 03-06). The editor then was Coleman. CHA 2945
         2:6 says this is an abridged edition of no. 03-06. Not attr.
         Howes L503; S. 34889. Shaw 3882 attr. to Charles Brock-
         den Brown.

03-17   A letter concerning the Ten Pound Court, in the City of New-
         York . . . By Mercer. New-York . . . 1803. 8vo. 38p.

         By James Cheetham.

         S. 12376; Jeff. 3326.

03-18   Letters addressed to the army . . . Year 1783 . . . Kingston . . .
         New York. 1803. 8vo. 19p.

         By John Armstrong?

         S. 40569; CHA 1491 3:1 so suggest. Shaw 3689.

03-19   The letters of the British spy . . . Richmond . . . 1803. 8vo.
         43p. 2nd ed. 88p.

         By William Wirt.

         S. 104875; Rich 2:43; Church 1297; Servies 1816; Howes
         W585; D.A.B. 20:420; Shaw 5606, 5607. (The letters by
         "An Inquirer" attr. to George Tucker in McLean pp. 54, 241.)

03-20   (Letter to Gabriel Jones dated July 20, 1803. Signed, Veritas.)
         Fol. 1 leaf.

         By Philip Grymes.

S. 98977; Jeff. 3305; Wise & Cronin 487.

03-21   Liberty in Louisiana; a comedy . . . Charleston. 1803.

By James Workman.

S. 105482; Shaw 5620; no copy seen. Second edition no. 04-30.

03-22   The Mississippi question fairly stated, and the views . . . of those who clamor for war, examined . . . By Camillus. Philadelphia . . . 1803. 8vo. 2p. l. 48p.

By William Duane.

Kress B4654; Cush. 1 p. 49; Jeff. 3471; Shaw 4112. Also attr. to his son William J. Duane, S. 21000; Howes D518.

03-23   Moll Carey. Song to be sung at the close of the Republican exercises . . . New Haven, March 9, 1803. Twelve stanzas.

By Theodore Dwight.

Shaw 4123; reprinted 1874 with annotation, S. 86891.

03-24   Monroe's embassy, or, the conduct of the Government, in relation to . . . Mississippi . . . Philadelphia . . . 1803. Signed, Poplicola. 8vo. 57p.

By Charles Brockden Brown.

B.A.L. 1506; Howes B832; Shaw 3883; Cronin & Wise, Monroe, 103. S. 50022 not attr.

03-25   Observations on the petitions from various merchants of Rhode-Island to the Congress . . . Newport . . . 1803. 4to. 34p.

By William Hunter.

S. 56544; Jeff. 3308; Shaw 4420.

03-26   Observations on the trial by jury . . . dangerous consequences of innovations . . . By an American . . . Strasburg . . . 1803. 8vo. 143(1)p.

By William Barton.

S. 3854; not attr. in S. 56570 or Shaw 4783. Compiler has copy noted in contemporary hand: "W. Barton Esq. of Lancaster".

03-27   Publications . . . difference of opinion between the governor and the council on their respective powers. Annapolis . . . 1803. 12mo. iv, 138p.

By Alexander Contee Hanson.

S. 66525; Jeff. 3329; D.A.B. 8:230; Shaw 4333; CHA 8905 2:4.

03-28   Reflections on the cession of Louisiana to the United States. By Sylvestris. Washington City . . . 1803. 8vo. 27p.

By St. George Tucker?

Davis p. 401. Howes L510: "possible author: Joseph Locke, but generally ascribed to St. George Tucker, or to William Stedman". S. 94100 not attr. Attr. to Tucker by Library of Congress.

03-29   A refutation of the charges made by . . . Veritas, against the character of Gabriel Jones . . . Winchester (1803). 4to. 32p.

By Gabriel Jones.

S. 98977+; Jeff. 3305 note; D.A.B. 10:170. See no. 03-20.

03-30   Remarks on the late infraction of treaty at New-Orleans. By Coriolanus. New-York . . . 1803. 8vo. 44p.

By William Stephens Smith.

S. 84903; Jeff. 3470; Howes S724; Shaw 5075; not attr. S. 16785.

03-31   Republican address to the freemen of Connecticut. Fellow citizens . . . [caption] (n.p. 1803). 8vo. 16p. Also edition with "Free Men".

By Alexander Wolcott?

S. 104980; Dex. 4 p. 82 (supposed author). Dated Aug. 30, 1803. Not attr. Shaw 4068. CHA 18588 1:2 attr. to Levi Ives, who was clerk.

03-32   Republican festival, proclamation and New Jerusalem. New Haven. (1803). Dated March 9, 1803. 8vo. 16p.

By David Austin.

S. 2402; Dex. 4 p. 96; Shaw 3702; D.A.B. 1:432.

03-33   To the freemen of the State of Connecticut. Fellow citizens ... (n.p. 1803). 8vo. 16p.

By Richard Alsop.

Shaw 3659. Not to be confused with Shaw 5180, by Uriah Tracy, Dex. 4 p. 65.

03-34   A view of certain proceedings in the two houses of the legislature ... new state bank ... Albany. 1803. 8vo. 24p.

By Samuel Stringer.

S. 92865; Shaw 5119.

03-35   A vindication of the measures of the present administration. By Algernon Sidney ... Washington ... 1803. 8vo. 20p.; Hartford, 8vo. 32p.; Portsmouth 8vo. 23p.; Trenton 4to. 16p.; Washington 8vo. 20p.; Wilmington 16mo. 36p.; Utica?

By Gideon Granger.

S. 28283; Dex. 4:548; Jeff. 3301; Howes G301; D.A.B. 7:484. See S. 80856, 99810.

03-36   Voyage d'un Allemand, au lac Onéida ... Traduit de l'Allemand ... Paris ... 1803. 24mo., 1p., l., 203p., 1pl.

By Sophie von La Roche.

CHA 16459 3:6; S. 100811+, that J. H. Campe (S. 10309) was the editor.

03-37   Vue de la colonie espagnole du Mississipi, ou des provinces de

Louisiane . . . Paris . . . 1803. 12mo., xx, 318, 5(1) (3)p.,
2maps.

By F. Berquin-Duvallon.

Clark, II, 79; Monaghan 206; S. 4962, 100859+; Jeff.
4075. The author appears as "éditeur". His name appears
on the title page of the 1804 edition, S. 100859+. Translated no. 06-40.

1804

04-01   An account of Louisiana . . . abstract of documents . . . London
         . . . 1804. 8vo. 44p.

         By Jacob Wagner.

         S. 42178 not attr. See no. 03-01.

04-02   An account of Louisiana, exhibiting a compendious sketch . . .
         Newbern . . . 1804. 14.6 cm. (2), 272, 68, (2)p.

         By François-Xavier Martin.

         Streeter 1579; Howes L493+. S. 42180 not attr.

04-03   An account of Louisiana, laid before Congress . . . November
         14, 1803 . . . Providence [1804] . 12mo. 72p.

         By Jacob Wagner.

         See no. 03-01. Not attr. S. 42179; Shaw 5646.

04-04   An address to the citizens of New Hampshire, on the approach-
         ing election of state officers. (1804). 11p.

         By   Ladd.

         Shaw 6609.

04-05   Address to the electors of New Hampshire. (Portsmouth 1804).
         Signed, Impartialis. 8vo. 14p.

         By William Plumer.

S. 63448; Cunningham 297n. 72; CHA 15623 1:7; Shaw
7071; Plumer p. 314-316; Turner 146, 351.

04-06   An address to the people of Maryland . . . By a citizen . . .
(Hagerstown?). 1804. 27p.

By R. Smith?

Attribution suggested in Beard, p. 464, note. S. 45066;
Bristol 227 not attr.

04-07   An address to the people of Massachusetts. (Boston 1804).
8vo. 22p.

By Barnabas Bidwell.

Shaw 5871; Dex. 4 p. 390; Brin. 8626; CHA 2225 3:7.

04-08   An appendix to Aristides's vindication of the Vice-President
. . . by a gentleman of North Carolina. (Richmond?) 1804.
8vo. 20p.

By William Peter Van Ness.

S. 98530+. Shaw 5718 not attr. Also an appendix to no.
04-25.

04-09   Behren's lie detected! (New York 1804). Broadside.

By Aaron Burr?

Mitchell p. 525: "Burr, or less probably someone acting for
him . . ." Shaw 5831 no attribution. See no. 04-47.

04-10   A brief account of the New-York hospital. New York . . .
1804. (4)72(i.e., 76)p.

By John Murray, Jr. or Thomas Eddy?

S. 54481; Austin 1792 citing S. Shaw 6922 (39p.) not attr.

04-11   British influence on the affairs of the United States. Boston
. . . 1804. Signed, Marcus. 8vo. 23p.

By Oliver Wolcott.

S. 104983; Shaw 7793; Dex. 4 p. 86; Howes W611; Wise
& Cronin 796; Beard 297.

04-12   The British spy . . . Letters, to a member of the British Parlia-
         ment . . . Newburyport . . . 1804. 16mo. iv(i)6-105p.

         By William Wirt.

         S. 104871; Shaw 7787; Kress B4869; CHA 2900 3:6.
         See no. 03-19.

04-13   The builder's universal price book . . . observations on erecting
         . . . buildings . . . Washington . . . 1804. 17.5 cm. vi(7)-44.

         By John Evans.

         Shaw 6263; Kress B4795.

04-14   Circular. New-York, March 14, 1804. Sir, the General Com-
         mittee of Republicans . . . [New York 1804] . Broadside.

         By DeWitt Clinton.

         Cunningham 151. Shaw 6021 not attr.

04-15   A collection of the facts and documents, . . . Death . . . Hamil-
         ton; with comments . . . By the Editor of The Evening Post.
         New York . . . 1804. 8vo. (4),238p. Also published in
         five separate parts.

         By William Coleman.

         S. 14311; Ford 94; CHA 4730 2:7; Shaw 6041.

04-16   A concise view . . . Clintonian party . . . Merchants Bank. By a
         Spectator. New-York. 1804. 8vo. 15p.

         By Oliver Wolcott?

         S. 104983+ (Wolcott was president of the bank, 1803-
         1804). Attr. to William W. Woolny in Hammond, Bray,
         "Banks and Politics in America", Princeton, Princeton Uni-
         versity Press, 1957, pp. 160, 760. S. 105212 Woolny; S.
         15121 not attr.

04-17   The Constitutionalist: addressed to men of all parties . . . By
         an American . . . Philadelphia . . . 1804. 8vo. 49p.

         By William Barton.

S. 3852, 16143; Shaw 5816; Cush. 1 p. 12; Halk. 1 p. 423.

04-18   A correct statement of the late melancholy affair of honor, between General Hamilton and Col. Burr . . . By Lysander.
New York . . . 1804. 8vo. 78p.

By Thomas Wills.

S. 104541; Ford 110; Tompk. Burr 111; Wandell p. 247;
Shaw 7777 with "?" Also attr. to William P. Van Ness S.
98528+; Cush. 1 p. 177; DuPuy 2421, noting that copyright issued to Wills. Howes W510 suggests Wills and notes
also Van Ness.

04-19   Count the cost. An address to the people of Connecticut . . .
by Jonathan Steadfast . . . Hartford . . . 1804. 8vo. 21(2)p.

By David Daggett.

S. 90846+; Shaw 6109; Dex. 4 p. 263; Brin. 8176; D.A.B.
5:27; CHA 5119 1:4; not attr. S. 15716.

04-20   A defence of the conduct of Commodore Morris during his
command in the Mediterranean . . . New York . . . 1804 . . .
8vo. 98(1)p. map.

By Richard Valentine Morris.

S. 50862; Shaw 6823; D.A.B. 13:219.

04-21   A defence of the measures of the administration of Thomas
Jefferson. By Curtius . . . Washington . . . 1804. 8vo. 136p.

By John Taylor.

S. 18070, 94488; Jeff. 3316; Howes T60; Shaw 7333;
CHA 5904 3:7; Simms 216.

04-22   A description of the Genesee Country. By Robert Munro.
New-York . . . 1804. 8vo. 16p., map; also 13p., map; also
two editions, anonymous, 16mo. 24p.

By Charles Williamson.

CHA 6034-35; Vail p. 449; S. 99573, 104441+; Howes
W493; CHA 15044 16p., with p. 15 misnumbered. See

no. 04-48 for substantially the same work.

04-23   An epitome of Mr. Forsyth's treatise . . . fruit trees . . . by an
         American farmer . . . Philadelphia 1804. 8vo. (5)2-186(6)p.,
         fifteen plates.

         By William Cobbett.

         Gaines 63b. See no. 03-09.

04-24   An Essay on the manufacturing interest of the United States
         . . . Philadelphia . . . 1804. 8vo. 32,xviip.

         By Tench Coxe.

         S. 17296; Cush. 1 p. 190; Shaw 6092. Not attr.
         S. 22964, Jeff. 3309.

04-25   An examination of the various charges exhibited against Aaron
         Burr, Esq. . . . views of his political opponents . . . By
         Aristides . . . (N.Y.) 1804. (4)116p. "Virginia Edition"
         1804, 59p. "Cheap edition" Feb., 1804, 56p.

         By William Peter Van Ness.

         S. 98530+; Tompk. Burr 103+; DuPuy 364; Howes V37.
         See earlier eds. no. 03-13.

04-26   The Hamiltoniad: or, an extinguisher for the royal faction of
         New-England . . . By Anthony Pasquin . . . Boston . . . (1804).
         8vo. 104p.

         By John M. Williams.

         S. 104279; Weg. 1207; Shaw 7766; Howes W464; Tompk.
         Burr 109; D.A.B. 20:271; Ford 106 has 64p.

04-27   Hamiltoniad; or, the effects of discord . . . By a young gentle-
         man of Philadelphia . . . Phila. 1804. 8vo. 40 l.(1)34-55p.

         By Joseph R. Hopkins.

         Ford 96; Tompk. Burr 50; Weg. 998; Wandell p. 126; Shaw
         6497; Shaw 6498 is 95p., but query.

04-28   A letter to Aaron Burr, Vice-President . . . on the baneful effects of duels . . . By Philanthropos . . . New-York . . . 1804. 8vo. 32p.

By William Ladd.

CHA 12091 3:3; Howes L10; Wandell p. 204; not attr. in S. 9427, or Ford 97 or Tompk. Burr 62.

04-29 Letters from London . . . Boston . . . 1804 . . . 312p.

By William Austin.

D.A.B. 1:441; Shaw 5745.

04-30 Liberty in Louisiana; a comedy . . . 2d ed. . . . Charleston . . . 1804. 16mo. vii(1), (5)-103, (1)p.

By James Workman.

S. 105482; Shaw 7804. See no. 03-21.

04-31 Life of Alexander Hamilton. Boston. 1804.

By John M. Williams?

Shaw 7767; D.A.B. 20:271. Ford 108 thought a spurious title. No copy known to MWA.

04-32 A memoir of the Moheagan Indians. Written in the year 1804. (Boston, 1804). 8vo. 27p.

By Abiel Holmes.

CHA 9425 2:6; Shaw 6489.

04-33 Mémoire présenté au Congrès des États-Unis d'Amérique par les habitans de la Louisiane. Nouvelle-Orléans . . . 1804. 33p.

By Edward Livingston.

Translated in 04-36; Shaw 6766 not attr.

04-34 Mémoires sur la Louisiane et la Nouvelle Orleans . . . Paris 1804. 8vo. (8)176p. tab.

By Charles E. P. Wante?

S. 101246; Howes W87; not attr. Streeter 1581; S. 42895; Monaghan 268 attr. to Boucher de la Richardière.

04-35   Memorial of the citizens and inhabitants of the Indiana Territory, praying for the interposition of Congress . . . Washington City . . . 1804. 6p.

By James May.

Shaw 6760. S. 34555 not attr. (date wrong).

04-36   Memorial presented by the inhabitants of Louisiana to the Congress . . . Translated from the French . . . Washington . . . 1804. 21p.

By Edward Livingston.

Hatcher, William B., Edward Livingston (Baton Rouge, 1940) pp. 112, 113; Malone v.4, p. 358; not attr. Shaw 7541; S. 42261; A. W. Greeley, Public Documents of the First Fourteen Congresses, p. 369.

04-37   Observations on the intended canal in Washington City. Washington. 1804. 24p.

By Thomas Law.

Shaw 6630.

04-38   Observations on the principles and operation of banking. By Anti-monopoly . . . (Philadelphia) 1804. 8vo. 21p., cover title.

By William Duane.

Kress B4790; Cush. 1 p. 17; Halk. 4 p. 223; Shaw 6194.

04-39   Observations upon . . . Mr. Jefferson's Notes on Virginia . . . tendency to subvert religion . . . New-York. 1804. 8vo. 32p.

By Clement C. Moore?

S. 50336; Swem 3764; Tompk. Jeff. 219; Shaw 6812; CHA 11449 2:2; also attr. to Nicholas Rogers S. 72717; Howes R416. D.A.B. 13:118 is undecided.

04-40   The opportunity; or, Reasons for an immediate alliance with
         St. Domingo . . . London . . . 1804. 8vo., viii, 156p.

         By James Stephen.

         CHA 20772 2:3; S. 57413, 91241+; Kress B4861.

04-41   Particulars of the late duel, fought at Hoboken, July 11, be-
         tween Aaron Burr and Alexander Hamilton . . . New York
         . . . 1804. 8vo. 32p.

         By William Coleman?

         Most of this is no. 04-15. Not attr. Tompk. Burr 69; Ford
         103; Shaw 6991.

04-42   A personal satire . . . written by a schoolmaster in the Eastern
         Country to his competitors . . . Boston . . . 1804. 12p.

         By Aza Humphrey.

         Shaw 6516 (corrected). S. 77885 not attr.

04-43   Political economy . . . In a letter to a friend. By W. T. . . .
         Washington . . . 1804. 8vo. 24p.

         By William Thornton.

         S. 95645; Cush. 1 p. 279; Shaw 7349; D.A.B. 18:506.

04-44   The Rainbow; First Series . . . Richmond . . . 1804. 8vo.
         (4)72p.

         By George Tucker (3 essays signed "x"), James Ogilvie,
         William Wirt, Thomas Ritchie and other Richmond citizens.

         McLean pp. 54, 55, 213n., 241. S. 67527, 104881+ attr. to
         William Wirt and friends. D.A.B. 20:420 attr. to Wirt.

04-45   The Sham-Patriot Unmasked . . . arts of demagogues . . . By
         Historicus. Peacham . . . 1804. 8vo. 81p.

         By Ezra Sampson.

         McCorison 755; Shaw 7228. See no. 02-29.

04-46   A Sketch of the character of Alexander Hamilton . . . Boston,

1804. 8vo. 15p.

By Fisher Ames.

Ford 93; S. 1301; Shaw 5706. Not attr. S. 29992; Shaw 7273. Reprinted substantially in "Works of Fisher Ames", Boston, 1809, pp. 282-90.

04-47   To the Electors of the State of New York . . . Poor Behrens! By a Young German. (New York, 1804). Broadside, 41.5x 38 cm.

By Herman Behrens?

Mitchell p. 760n. 19 says "probably"; E. Supp. B10914 (dates 1799); not attr. Shaw 7814. See no. 04-09.

04-48   A view of the present situation of the western parts . . . New-York . . . Genesee Country . . . Frederick-Town . . . 1804. 12mo. 23p.

By Charles Williamson.

Vail p. 449; Howes W493; CHA 6035 1:2; S. 99573, 104444+(?); Bristol 315 ("supposed author"); Shaw 7771. See no. 04-22.

04-49   A vindication of the rights of the New England Mississippi Land Company . . . City of Washington, 1804. 8vo. 109p.

By Gideon Granger.

Dex. 4 p. 548. S. 52708, 99829+ not attr. Appears also as annex to "Memorial of the agents of the New England Mississippi Land Company . . ." (1804); Shaw 6879. The memorialists were Granger and Perez Morton.

04-50   William Judd's address to the people of . . . Connecticut. (New Haven) 1804. 8vo. 24p.

By Abraham Bishop?

Dex. 4:23; attr. to Judd in S. 36846; Shaw 6576. See Purcell, p. 262-4.

1805

05-01 The address of the Society of Constitutional Republicans . . .
10th of June 1805 . . . Philadelphia . . . 1805. 8vo. 28p.

By Alexander James Dallas.

Jeff. 3338; Walters, p. 138; Tolles, p. 253; D.A.B. 5:38;
Higginbotham p. 92; not attr. in S. 401; Shaw 8246.

05-02 An address to the citizens of New Hampshire; By the Author
. . . 1805. 12mo. 31p.

By Thomas Cogswell.

S. 52793.

05-03 Address to the inhabitants of Marblehead . . . very bad police
. . . (n.p. 1805?). 12mo. 12p.

By William Reed.

S. 68593; NYHS 94.

05-04 An address to the people of Massachusetts. February, 1805.
(favoring Sullivan, Republican). 8vo. 24p.

By Barnabas Bidwell.

Dex. 4 p. 390; Shaw 8019; CHA 2226 1:1. S. 45605 not
attr.

05-05 The American Nepos . . . lives of . . . men who have contributed
to . . . America. Balt. . . . 1805. 12mo. p.(16)384, port.

By James J. Wilmer.

S. 1166, 104564+; Howes W513.

05-06 An Answer to the questions why are you a Federalist . . . 1805.
1805. 8vo. 22p.

By Josiah Quincy.

S. 67206; Brin. 8626; Shaw 9227; CHA 7019 1:2.

05-07 An appeal to the old whigs of New-Hampshire. Subscribed "An

Old Whig. February – 1805". 8vo. 16p.

By Daniel Webster.

S. 102255+; Turner 157n. S. 52801 not attr.; S. 63449 attr. to William Plumer.

05-08   An Argument upon the justice . . . detaining all ships bound to the Ports of Spain freighted with treasure or warlike stores . . . London . . . 1805. 63p.

By Edward Cooke?

So attr. on compiler's copy. Not Sabin nor Halk.

05-09   Considerations on the Choice of Public Rulers. New York . . . 1805. 8vo., vi, 156p.

By Thomas S. Arden?

So indicated on compiler's copy in later hand. He was the copyright holder. Not attr. in Shaw 8243; S. 15974.

05-10   A defence of the measures of the administration of Thomas Jefferson . . . Providence . . . 1805. 8vo. 88p.

By John Taylor.

Shaw 9454; D.A.B. 18:332; S. 94488. See no. 04-21.

05-11   The defence of Young and Minns, printers to the State . . . Boston . . . 1805. 8vo. (9)6-68p.

By Alexander Young?

Shaw 9778; not attr. S. 106131.

05-12   Democracy unveiled; or, tyranny stripped of the garb of patriotism. By Christopher Caustic, L.L.D. . . . Boston . . . 1805. 12mo. viii, 220p. Plus second edition, same.

By Thomas Green Fessenden.

S. 24212; Tompk. Jeff. 69; Weg. 957; Brin. 6857; Gilman p. 92; D.A.B. 6:347.

05-13   Discourses on Davila. A series of papers, on political history

... By an American citizen ... Boston ... 1805. 8vo. 248p.

By John Adams.

S. 239; Cronin & Wise, Adams 29. See Smith, P., Vol. 2, pp. 797-802.

05-14   Facts and arguments respecting the great utility of ... inland navigation ... By a friend to national industry ... Phila. ... 1805. 8vo., 61(1)p., fold., map.

By Turner Camac or William Blodget.

Attr. to Camac S. 10096; Howes C76; Shaw 8418 corrected; attr. to Blodget S. 5959; Howes B539; attr. to both, Kress B4911.

05-15   The first settlers of Virginia, an historical novel ... the countenance of the country and its natural productions ... New York ... 1805. 12mo., xii(13)-284p.

By John Davis.

CHA 5824 1:2; S. 18849; Shaw 8302.

05-16   The flying roll; or the miscellaneous writings of Redemptio ... Windsor ... 1805. 12mo. 108p.

By Richard R. Smith.

S. 83790; McCorison 809; Shaw 9382. Gilman p. 96 not attr.

05-17   Interesting detail of the operations of the American fleet in the Mediterranean ... Springfield ... (1805). 8vo. 31p.

By William Eaton.

S. 21743; Howes E31; CHA 6473 3:2; Shaw 8366; Shaw 6215 is same (1804).

05-18   Letters concerning the general health ... by a householder ... New York ... 1805. 8vo. (3)52p.

By Samuel Miles Hopkins.

S. 32961; Austin 947; NYHS 58; Dex. 4:715; Shaw 8641.
S. 73016 attr. in the alternative to Nicholas Romayne.

05-19 Letters from Europe during a tour through Switzerland . . . by
       a native of Pennsylvania. Philadelphia . . . 1805. 2v. xv(2)
       10-524; xi(2)2-155, 160-346, 353-472p.

       By Joseph Sansom.

       Shaw 9311; LCP 652; Palmer pp. 403, 404.

05-20 Letters of Decius, to the members of the legislature of the
       Indiana Territory . . . Louisville . . . 1805. 8vo. 46p.

       By John Randolph?

       Jeff. 3342; Howes I26(44p.); S. 19148, 40609 semble;
       Shaw 8309 not attr.

05-21 The letters of the British spy . . . The 3rd ed. Richmond . . .
       1805. 8vo. 128p.

       By William Wirt.

       CHA 12536 3:2; Shaw 9750. See no. 04-12.

05-22 A Letter to a Federalist, in reply . . . present administration.
       February, 1805. (Portsmouth, N.H.). 8vo. 31p.

       By Thomas Elwyn.

       S. 22375; Tompk. Jeff. 60; Johnston p. 34; Jeff. 3324;
       Wise & Cronin 429; Shaw 8388, 8777. See no. 05-25.

05-23 Observations on the South Carolina memorial upon the
       subject of duelling . . . by Postumus. n.p. 1805. 12mo.
       32p.

       By Charles Cotesworth Pinckney?

       Trumbull 416. Not attr. S. 64571, 87905; Shaw 9048.

05-24 162 - Vs - 14. (1805). Subscribed, Alexander Wolcott, State
       Manager. Dated 1805. 8vo. 8p.

       By Alexander Wolcott.

       S. 104979; Shaw 9758.

05-25   A parody on . . . a late pamphlet . . . "A Letter to a Federalist"
        . . . By Vernon H. Quincey . . . Portsmouth . . . 1805. 8vo.
        viii(1)10-47p.

        By Jonathan M. Sewall.

        S. 79401; Cush. 1 p. 244; Shaw 9339; Francis P. Harper,
        Catalogue 67, No. 508. Shaw 9226 attr. to V. H. Quincey (?).

05-26   Proposal for calling a convention. Philadelphia . . . 1805. 8vo.
        30p.

        By Nathaniel B. Boileau?

        See Higginbotham, pp. 81, 82; not attr. S. 60437; Shaw
        9128.

05-27   Reflections on the cause of the Louisianians, respectfully sub-
        mitted by their agents. (Washington? 1805). 17p. blank
        leaf.

        The "agents" were Pierre Derbigny, Jean Noel Destréhan
        and Pierre Sauvé.

        CHA 18487 1:3; not attr. S. 42288 (1804); Shaw 4958
        (1803), 9237 (1805).

05-28   Remarks, occasioned by . . . a memorial to Congress . . .
        Washington City . . . 1805. 8vo. 35p.

        By William Cowan?

        It is signed "the agent of the Virginia Yazoo Co." Cowan
        was agent in 1803 (S. 100571). Not attr. S. 69389; Shaw
        9676.

05-29   Sampson against the Philistines, or the reformation of lawsuits
        . . . Philadelphia . . . 1805. 8vo. v, 98, xxiiip.; also iv(1)6-
        96p.; also German edition, Ephrata, 1805.

        By Jesse Higgins or William Sampson.

        Attr. Higgins Reed 2733; Shaw 9307 (as corrected). Ap.
        Cyc. 5:383 and CHA 19311 1:7 attr. to Sampson; S.
        20994+ attr. William Duane; not attr. Shaw 9362; S.
        75924. Compiler has copy noted "By Jesse Higgins" in
        early hand.

05-30   The Sham-Patriot Unmasked . . . the fatally successful arts of
          Demagogues . . . Concord . . . 1805. 8vo. iv(1)6-48p.; also
          5th ed. Haverhill, iv(1)6-47p.

          By Ezra Sampson.

          S. 75930, 79740; Shaw 9305, 06; CHA 19310 2:6. See
          no. 02-29.

05-31   Steady habits vindicated: or a serious remonstrance to the
          people of Connecticut, . . . By a friend to the public welfare
          . . . Hartford . . . 1805. 8vo. 20p.

          By David Daggett.

          S. 90848+; Dex. 4 p. 263; Shaw 8284; not attr. S. 15859.

05-32   Walter Kennedy: An American tale . . . London . . . 1805. 12
          mo., vii, 192p., 2l.

          By John Davis.

          CHA 5824 2:5; S. 101204. Including Kaskaskia Indian
          vocabulary.

05-33   War in disguise; or, the frauds of the neutral flags . . . London
          . . . 1805. 8vo. iv, 215p. (two issues); second ed. 12mo.
          vii, 252p.

          By James Stephen.

          Kress B4985,6; S. 5827; S. 91246; Jeff. 2117, 2809;
          Howes S937; Bemis 101; Halk. 6 p. 207 says also attr. to
          John Brown, of Yarmouth.

1806

06-01   An address to the freemen of Connecticut. Hartford . . . 1806.
          8vo. 7p.

          By Noah Webster, Jr.

          S. 102334; Dex. 4 p. 74; Skeel p. 524 no. 8; not attr. S.
          15645.

06-02 An address to the people of the County of Franklin. Middle-
       bury, Vermont . . . 1806. 12mo. 10p.

       By John White.

       S. 103407; Gilman p. 329; McCorison 884.

06-03 Address to the six nations . . . New York . . . 1806. 8p.

       By John Norton.

       Shaw 11043; 11439.

06-04 All impressments unlawful and inadmissible . . . Philadelphia
       . . . 12p.; also Boston . . . 12p. (1806).

       By James Madison.

       Jeff. 3355, Philadelphia; Shaw 10775, Boston; CHA 9808
       2:5. Dated 1807, Shaw 12363; 1808, Shaw 15479, 80; and
       1810, Shaw 20633. S. 34409 not attr.

06-05 American arguments for British rights . . . republication of . . .
       letters of Phocion . . . London . . . 1806. 8vo. xii,74p.

       By William L. Smith.

       S. 84818; Kress B5121; Ford preface; D.A.B. 17:366.
       S. 29948 attr. to Alexander Hamilton, in error per Ford.
       See no. 06-28.

06-06 An answer to War in Disguise . . . concerning neutral trade . . .
       New York . . . 1806. 8vo. 76p. Also London, same
       collation.

       By Gouverneur Morris or Rufus King.

       S. 50827; Jeff. 2118; Shaw 50698; Kress B5080,81; and
       Brin. 4894 cite Morris. In no. 08-44 the author writes (p.
       2): "attributed by those who have the best means of know-
       ing, to His Excellency Rufus King, Esq." Howes M825:
       "More probably by Rufus King." However, not mentioned
       in Robert Ernst, "Rufus King" (1968).

06-07 The complete Justice of the Peace . . . by a gentleman of the
       profession . . . Dover, N.H. . . . 1806. 8vo. (8)431p.

By Moses Hodgdon.

Shaw 10569.

06-08   Considerations on the public expediency of a bridge . . .
        Boston . . . Boston . . . 1806. 8vo. 33p.

        By William Tudor?

        S. 6600, 97401+; Shaw 11484. Has been attr. to H. G. Otis,
        but not by S. E. Morison, his biographer.

06-09   Darkness at noon . . . great solar eclipse . . . by an inhabitant of
        Boston . . . Boston . . . 1806. 12mo. 36p., including plate;
        plus second ed., same, 34p.

        By Andrew Newell?

        S. 18580, "probably". Newell was one of the printers.
        Shaw 10253, 54 not attr.

06-10   Democracy unveiled; or, tyranny stripped of the garb of
        patriotism. By Christopher Caustic . . . Third ed. New York
        . . . 1806, 2 vols. 12mo. 179, 238p.

        By Thomas Green Fessenden.

        S. 24212; Shaw 50676. See no. 05-12.

06-11   Economica: A statistical manual . . . Washington . . . 1806. 8vo.
        viii, 202, xivp.

        By Samuel Blodget, Jr.

        S. 5956; Howes B537; Shaw 10004. The author placed his
        name on page 3.

06-12   An examination of the British doctrine, which subjects to cap-
        ture a neutral trade . . . (Philadelphia, 1806). 8vo. 204p.;
        London 1806, 8vo. (2)200p.

        By James Madison.

        Jeff. 2116; S. 43707; Kress B5065,66; Brant 1800-09, pp.
        297-301; Cronin & Wise, Madison, 10; Bemis 104; Halk. 2,
        p. 230 is London ed., with a letter to Lord Mulgrave on
        neutral trade (by James Monroe, Cronin & Wise, Monroe, 11).
        Brant dates first printing January, 1806.

06-13   Examination of the memorial of the owners . . . ship the New
Jersey . . . as presented to the Senate . . . by a friend to truth
and justice . . . Philadelphia 1806. 146p.

By John Armstrong?

Attr. to Armstrong in early hand on MBAt. copy. Not attr.
S. 23361; Shaw 10378. The memorial was adverse to Armstrong.

06-14   The first settlers of Virginia, an historical novel . . . the countenance of the country and its natural productions . . . New
York . . . 1806. xii (1)14-284p.; also 1p.,1,(1), vi-xii, (1)
14-284p.

By John Davis.

CHA 5824 1:3, 4; S. 18849; Shaw 10259. See no. 05-15.

06-15   History of the war between the United States and Tripoli . . .
Salem . . . 1806. 12mo. 144p.

By Stephen C. Blyth.

S. 6050; S. 96993+; Brin. 4972; Howes B560; Tapley p.
402; Shaw 10009.

06-16   An Impartial enquiry . . . Governor Lewis . . . The Merchant's
Bank . . . By Politicus . . . New-York . . . 1806. 8vo. iv(1)
6-116, xxxvp.

By James Cheetham.

Jeff. 3345. S. 63828 suggests Cheetham. CHA 4277 3:1;
Kress B5026; Shaw 10123 "supposed author". See Hammond 218-221; 332-335. See no. 06-29.

06-17   An inquiry into the effects of our foreign carrying trade . . .
By Columella . . . New York 1806. 8vo. 61p.

By Clement C. Moore.

S. 50335; Cush. 1 p. 65; Shaw 10893; Kress B5078.

06-18   An inquiry into the present state of the foreign relations of
the union . . . 1806. Philadelphia. 8vo. 183p. signed,

Independent American.

By Edmund Morford?

Not attr. S. 34815; Jeff. 3353; Wise & Cronin 512; Shaw 10615. Charles L. Woodward cat. 32 no. 659 is copy endorsed: "By Edmund Morford, born 1787 died 1833."

06-19 An inquiry into the state of the nation, at the commencement of the present administration . . . 3d ed. . . . London 1806. 8vo. 2p. l. 219,xviiip.

By Henry Peter Brougham, Lord.

Kress B5018; Edinburgh 1:547: S. 25367 attr. to Henry R. V. Fox.

06-20 Letters of Marcus addressed to DeWitt Clinton. (Poughkeepsie 1806?). 8vo. 16p.

By William Peter Van Ness.

S. 98531. Attr. to Matthew L. Davis in Shaw 10261, but see no. 10-19.

06-21 A letter to the honourable John Bacon, Esq. . . . Boston (1806). 8vo. 7(1)p.

By James Lovell.

Sibley 14:47; Shaw 10749. Reprinted over his name Shaw 15453.

06-22 A memoir, containing an examination of the British doctrine, which subjects to capture a neutral trade . . . Washington . . . 1806. 8vo. 202p.

By James Madison.

Jeff. 3354; Cronin & Wise, Madison 33. S. 47497 not attr. See no. 06-12.

06-23 Memorial of the inhabitants of the town of Salem . . . Massachusetts. January 30, 1806. City of Washington 1806. 8vo. 18p.

By Joseph Story.

S. 92309; not attr. S. 75673; Shaw 11624.

06-24   Memorial of the Merchants of Baltimore, on the violation of
         our neutral rights . . . Baltimore . . . 1806. 8vo. 49p.

         By William Pinkney.

         D.A.B. 14:627. Shaw 10854 not attr.; S. 62969 attributes,
         has Washington as place of publication.

06-25   Message from the President . . . transmitting a Memorial of the
         merchants of Baltimore on the violation of our neutral
         rights. January 29th 1806 . . . City of Washington . . .
         1806. 8vo. 34(2)p.

         The memorial is by William Pinkney.

         Wheaton p. 50, 372. See preceding entry.

06-26   Narrative of the adventures of an American Navy officer . . .
         New York . . . 1806. 12mo. 270p.

         By Nathaniel Fanning.

         S. 23783, 51795; Shaw 10385; D.A.B. 6:268; Howes F29;
         Streeter 809.

06-27   Notes on the United States of America. Philadelphia . . . 1806.
         8vo. 48p.

         By Gouverneur Morris.

         Jeff. 3349; Kress B5082; Shaw 10908; S. 50829 (1816);
         Rich 2 p. 25.

06-28   The numbers of Phocion . . . published in the Charleston
         Courier in 1806 . . . Charleston. 8vo. 70p.

         By William L. Smith.

         S. 84828; D.A.B. 17:366; Wolfe 206-9; Rogers 365; Shaw
         11388.

06-29   Observations on the conduct of Governor Lewis . . . bribery . . .
         Merchant's Bank . . . by Politicus . . . New York 1806. 8vo.
         23p.

By James Cheetham.

Cush. 2 p. 122; Halk. 4 p. 219. S. 63829 suggests Cheetham. See no. 06-16.

06-30   Observations on the improvements of the City of New York
         . . . New York. 1806. 8vo. 8p.

         By John S. Hunn.

         S. 33835; NYHS 60; not attr. Shaw 11001.

06-31   Observations on the speech of the Hon. John Randolph . . .
         By the author of War in Disguise . . . New York . . . 1806.
         8vo. 43p.

         By James Stephen.

         S. 91241; Kress B5125; Swem 5302; Shaw 11408. See no.
         06-36.

06-32   A poem on liberty . . . commencement of Union College . . .
         Albany . . . 1806. 8vo. 12p.

         By Teunis A. Van Vechten.

         Weg. 1181; S. 63586, 98582+; Shaw 11752.

06-33   Prospectus of a national institution to be established in the
         United States. Washington . . . 1806. 8vo. 44p.

         By Joel Barlow.

         S. 3429; Dex. 4 p. 14; B. Ath. p. 237; B.A.L. 905; Shaw
         9922.

06-34   The Quid mirror. The first part . . . Philadelphia . . . 1806. 8vo.
         24p.; New York . . . 1806. 8vo. 33p.

         By William Dickson?

         Tolles 276; Walters 142. "promptly reissued in Philadelphia"
         . . . Letters of Benjamin Rush, edited by L. H. Butterfield, p.
         934, note 2. Not attr. S. 67168; Jeff. 3426; Shaw 11233, 4.

06-35   The sixth of August or the Litchfield Festival. An address . . .
         Dated (at end) September 1st, 1806. 8vo. 16p.

By Tapping Reeve.

Purcell 434; Wandell 216; CHA 5143 1:6; not attr. in S. 41474, 81493; Shaw 11366.

06-36   The speech of the Hon. J. Randolph . . . with an introduction by the author of "War in Disguise". London . . . 1806. 8vo. (4),xlv,(1),31(1)p. Editions with 21 lines of advertising or with three. Some have extra leaf after p. xlv.

Introduction by James Stephen.

S. 67839; Halk. 4 p. 224. No. 06-31 is New York reprint of the introduction.

06-37   Statements concerning the Blodget Canal at Amoskeag Falls, on Merrimac River . . . [Boston?] 1806. 8vo. 8p.

By Samuel Blodget.

Shaw 10005, mistakenly attr. to his son, Samuel Blodget, Jr.

06-38   The study and practice of the law considered . . . Portland . . . 1806. 364p.

By John Raithby.

Shaw 11238.

06-39   Thoughts on the subject of naval power in the United States . . . Phila. . . . 1806. 8vo. 35p.

By Tench Coxe.

S. 17306, 95727; Howes C832; Shaw 10223.

06-40   Travels in Louisiana and the Floridas, in the year 1802 . . . translated from the French . . . by John Davis . . . New York . . . 1806. 12mo., viii, 181p.

By F. Berquin-Duvallon.

S. 4965; CHA 5824 2:7; Clark II, 79(3); Monaghan 208. See no. 03-37 for French original.

06-41   Van Tromp lowering his peak . . . plea for the Baptists . . . Danbury. 1806. 36p.

By John Leland.

Shaw 10715; D.A.B. 11:161; Purcell pp. 76, 432; M. Louise Greene, "The Development of Religious Liberty in Connecticut" (Boston 1905), p. 429, dates 1803.

06-42 A Vindication of the doctrine advocated by John Randolph . . . By Epaminondas. New York. 1806. 8vo. 36p.

By Augustus B. Woodward?

S. 105157; Wandell 96; not attr. Shaw 10363.

06-43 War in disguise; or, the frauds of the neutral flags . . . New York. January, 1806. 8vo. vip., l., 215p. (2 eds.); also London vip. (3)10-228p. (2 eds.).

By James Stephen.

S. 91246,47; Kress B5126-29. See no. 05-33.

06-44 Who shall be Governor, Strong or Sullivan? . . . the Sham-Patriot unmasked . . . 1806. 8vo. 30p.

By Ezra Sampson.

Shaw 11322 has Moses Sampson; S. 103846 not attr. Reprint of no. 02-29.

1807

07-01 An account of a voyage up the Mississippi . . . 1805-1806. (Washington 1807?). 8vo. 68p. map.

Nicholas King or Samuel L. Mitchill, compiler. From Zebulon M. Pike journal.

Howes P372; Streeter 1774. Under Pike: S. 62835; Shaw 13393 (also Shaw 11168, 1806).

07-02 The British Treaty. (Philadelphia 1807). 8vo. 86p.

By Charles Brockden Brown or Gouverneur Morris.

Attr. to Brown B.A.L. 1511; Shaw 12217; S. 8457+
Brown supposed author; not attr. S. 8126; attr. to Morris
S. 50832. See no. 08-10.

07-03 Circular to the people of Wake County (Raleigh, N.C., 1807).
12p.

By Calvin Jones.

Shaw 12844.

07-04 Concessions to America the bane of Britain . . . London 1807.
8vo. 63p.

By Joseph Marryat.

S. 44703; Kress B5224.

07-05 Copies and abstracts of certain letters and official documents
(New Orleans, 1807). 8vo. 30p.

By James Workman.

S. 105478. Concerning James Wilkinson.

07-06 Dangers of the country . . . Philadelphia . . . 1807. 8vo. 2p.,
l., 142p.; Charleston . . . 142p.; London xvi,163p.; iv,
227p.

By James Stephen.

S. 18487, 91235+; CHA 20772 1:3,4; Shaw 13642,43;
Halk. 2 p. 6. S. 18487 mentions John Brown as possible
author.

07-07 The Echo. Printed at the porcupine press by Pasquin Petronius.
[N.Y.] 1807. 8vo. (16)331(11)p. 8 plates.

By Richard Alsop, Theodore Dwight and Lemuel Hopkins,
principally.

S. 966, 21778; B.A.L. 1315; Weg. 1266; D.A.B. 9:215.
Some copies have brown plates.

07-08 An Essay on the rights and duties of nations . . . affair of the
Chesapeake. By an American. Boston . . . 1807. 8vo. 62p.

By David Everett.

S. 23242; Brin. 5071; Kress B5180; Shaw 12526; D.A.B. 6:223.

07-09   Examen de la sentence rendue dans la cause entre Jean Gravier et la Ville de la Nouvelle-Orléans. A la Nouvelle-Orléans . . . 1807. 4to. 22p.

By Louis C. E. Moreau de Lislet.

Jeff. 3483; Shaw 13120. French original of no. 09-14.

07-10   An examination of the conduct of Great Britain respecting neutrals . . . Phila. . . . 1807. By Juriscola. 8vo. 72p.

By Tench Coxe.

Kress B5167; Shaw 12364; Howes C830. S. 43708 and Shaw 12972 attr. James Madison; not Cronin & Wise, Madison, nor Brant. See no. 08-23.

07-11   Experience the test of government . . . laws of Pennsylvania . . . Philadelphia . . . 1807. 8vo. 60p.

By William Duane or Isaac Weaver, Jr.

Attr. to Duane S. 20986; Shaw 12469. S. 102203+ reports a copy noted "by Isaac Weaver"; CHA 6347 1:5. Shaw 14179 attr. to Weaver cancelled in corrections.

07-12   A faithful picture of the political situation of New Orleans . . . (New Orleans) 1807. 8vo. (4)38p.

By James Workman?

S. 105480+; Howes W677. See no. 08-24. Also attr. to Edward Livingston; S. 53325 not attr.

07-13   A few observations on the government of the State of Rhode Island . . . Providence 1807. 8vo. 18p.

By Benjamin Cowell.

Shaw 12357. S. 24235 not attr.

07-14   The ghost of Baron Steuben . . . mischief of a standing army . . .

(Salem 1807). 8vo. 8p. Caption title. Signed: Timothy Crabshaw.

By Oliver Hillhouse Prince.

CHA 8104 1:3; Shaw 13437.

07-15 The go-between, or two edged sword. Being an impartial address to the citizens . . . By a gentleman from South Carolina . . . (Signed, Hornet) . . . New York. 1807. 8vo. 37p.

By Mr. Devot?

CHA 9505 2:5. Shaw 12670 not attr.

07-16 Military reflections, on four modes of defence, for the United States . . . translated . . . Baltimore . . . 1807. 42p.

By Maximilian Godefroy.

Bristol 538; Shaw 12671; not attr. S. 46998.

07-17 A narrative of facts relative to the conduct of some of the members of the Legislature of Pennsylvania, professing to be Democrats . . . Philadelphia, 1807. 8vo. 16p. Two editions, dated May and June, respectively.

By Abner Lacock.

Higginbotham 139, 354; not attr. S. 60268; Shaw 13168.

07-18 New reasons for abolishing the slave trade . . . last section of "the dangers of the country" . . . London . . . 1807. 8vo. 67p.

By James Stephen.

S. 91240; Kress B5267. See no. 07-06.

07-19 Old England and America, against France and all Europe . . . by Patrioticus. London, 1807. 8vo. 44p.?

By William P. Russell.

S. 74294; Halk. 4 p. 244.

07-20 On the maritime rights of Great Britain . . . signed Vindex. Part 1-2. London . . . 1807. 2 parts, 8vo., 19, 59p.

By Sir Frederick Morton Eden.

CHA 6520 2:1; Kress B5178; S. 99777. See S. 21823 for editions naming the author.

07-21   Peace without dishonour—war without hope . . . the Chesapeake . . . By a Yankee Farmer. Boston . . . 1807. 8vo. 43p.; London . . . 1807. 8vo. 43p.

By John Lowell.

S. 42455; Tompk. Jeff. 208; Shaw 12947; Cush. 1 p. 311 attr. to Lowell; Cush. 2 p. 6 attr. to Rufus King. London edition by "An American Farmer", CHA 11929 1:3.

07-22   The picture of New York . . . Traveller's Guide . . . New York . . . 1807. 12mo. (8),223p., Plan; also (15)216p.

By Samuel L. Mitchill.

Kress B5229,30; S. 49746; Howes M703; Shaw 13104.

07-23   A plain tale . . . justifying the character of General Wilkinson . . . By a Kentuckian . . . New York 1807. 8vo. 24p.

By Charles Winterfield?

Howes W431 (possibly); Jacobs 348 (with ?); not attr. S. 63237; Shaw 13399.

07-24   The plot discovered. By Marcus . . . Poughkeepsie . . . 1807. 8vo. 12p.

By William Peter Van Ness.

S. 98532. Attr. to Matthew L. Davis S. 18866; Shaw 12399 and Jeff. 3395; not attr. Tompk. Burr 76. Reprints no. 06-20.

07-25   The political farrago, or a miscellaneous review of the politics of the United States . . . Mammoth cheese . . . By Peter Dobbins, Esq. . . . Brattleboro . . . 1807. 8vo. 59p.

By William Fessenden?

S. 24221; McCorison 920; Cush. 1 p. 82; Shaw 12563.

07-26   Politics for American farmers . . . compared with . . . British monarchy . . . Washington city . . . 1807. 12mo. (2)200p.; also 8vo. (2)96p.

By William Duane.

S. 20991; Kress B5177; Johnston p. 35; Tompk. Jeff. 56; Shaw 12470,1. Not in William Duane, by Allen C. Clark. Washington. W. F. Roberts Co. 1905.

07-27   A short review of the late proceedings at New Orleans; . . . By Agrestis . . . South Carolina, 1807. 8vo. 42p., l.; also Richmond . . . 1807. 35p.

By Joseph Alston.

S. 80684,5; Howes A176; Wandell p. 11; Shaw 11972,3. Tompk. Burr 4 has John Alston but refers to Joseph Alston.

07-28   Six letters on the intrigues, apostacy and ambition of Doctor Michael Leib . . . By Veritas. (Philadelphia) 1807. 8vo. 24p.

By John Binns?

Higginbotham 140, 141. Not attr. S. 98981; Shaw 14113.

07-29   A slight view of the world. Taken July 4th, 1807. (Bennington, 1807). Broadside.

By Anthony Haswell.

Shaw 12730; Spargo 217; McCorison 927.

07-30   Solid reasons for continuance of war . . . advising . . . firm union between England and America . . . By Patrioticus . . . (London) 1807. 8vo. 44p., map.

By William P. Russell.

S. 74295; Halk. 4 p. 244; Kress B5251. Reprint of no. 07-19.

07-31   The steady habits of Connecticut, versified . . . Danbury, 1807.

By Isaac Hilliard.

Howard 438; Shaw 12751.

07-32   A summary of most important measures which have been be-
         fore us . . . the foreign relations of this country . . . (Washing-
         ton? 1807). 7p.

         By William B. Burwell.

         Shaw 12254.

07-33   To the freemen of Vermont. (Bennington, 1807). Broadside.

         By Anthony Haswell?

         Spargo 218 so indicates; Shaw 13710 not attr.

07-34   To the people of the United States. Philadelphia 1807. 8vo.
         (2)145p. 10 folding tables included.

         By William Maclure.

         S. 43556, 97944; Jeff. 2684; Shaw 12968; D.A.B. 12:135;
         Kress B5217.

07-35   The trial of Charles Vattier . . . by two gentlemen of law-knowl-
         edge . . . Cincinnati . . . 1807. lvii,154p.

         By George Turner?

         S. 97484. Shaw 13734 not attr.

07-36   Voyages dans l'intérieur de la Louisiane, de la Floride . . . 1802-
         1806 . . . Paris . . . 1807. 3 vols. 8vo. (4),xii, 346port.; (4),
         511, map; xii,551p.

         By Claude C. Robin.

         Monaghan 1247; Howes R362; S. 72039.

07-37   War in disguise; or, the frauds of the neutral flags . . . fifth edi-
         tion . . . London . . . 1807. 8vo. (4)iii-xxiv,124, 129-224,
         221-252p.

         By James Stephen.

         S. 91246. See no. 06-43.

07-38   Washington und die Amerikanische Revolution . . . Giesen (sic)
         1807. 16mo. (2)280p.

By Josias Ludwig Gosch.

S. 101896; Baker 62 has 478p.

07-39   Washington und die französische Revolution . . . Giessen . . .
        1807. 8vo.

        By Josias Ludwig Gosch.

        S. 101898.

1808

08-01   Address of the State Committee . . . to the citizens of Pennsyl-
        vania. Dated, Philadelphia, July 25, 1808. 8vo. 10p.

        By Michael Leib.

        S. 39888. Not attr. Shaw 14859.

08-02   An address to the citizens of Massachusetts, on . . . national
        distresses. By a fellow-sufferer. Boston 1808. 8vo. 13p.

        By John Park.

        S. 58627; Cush. 1 p. 101; Kress B5418; Shaw 15846.

08-03   Address to the freemen of the counties of Wayne . . . Newbern,
        N.C. . . . 1808. 17p.

        By William Gaston.

        Shaw 15089. For reply see no. 08-41.

08-04   An address to the independent electors of Franklin County . . .
        Frankfort, Ky. . . . 1808. 8vo. 16p.

        By Humphrey Marshall.

        Jillson p. 40; Shaw 15496.

08-05   An address to the people of New England. By Algernon Sidney
        . . . Washington . . . 1808. 8vo. 38p., l; also 24p.

By Gideon Granger.

S. 28281; Dex. 4-548; CHA 3627 2:5; Jeff. 3462; Johnston p. 35; Shaw 15145-7; D.A.B. 7:484; Howes G300; attr. to Benjamin Watkins Leigh in S. 39911; Cush. 1 p. 278; Wise & Cronin 474.

08-06   Adresse au Conseil Legislatif du Territoire d'Orléans. Nouvelle-Orléans . . . 1808. 16p.

By Julien de Lalande Poydras.

Jeff. 3485; Shaw 15990. S. 53303 not attr.

08-07   Aristides, or a series of papers on the presidential election . . . 1808 . . . Charleston . . . (3)6-75p.

By Langdon Cheves.

Shaw 14683; Turnbull 438.

08-08   The Barber's shop, kept by Sir David Razor . . . Salem . . . 1808. 8vo. 64p.

By John S. Appleton.

Tapley 410. D.A.B. 18:102 that attribution to Isaac Story is incorrect.

08-09   Biographical memoirs of the illustrious General George Washington . . . Philadelphia . . . 1808. 18mo. 108p.

By John Corry.

S. 101778; Shaw 14783. An abridgement of Corry's "Life", London 1800.

08-10   The British Treaty. With an appendix . . . London reprinted . . . 1808. 8vo. 147(1)7p.; plus second edition (2)147(1)7p.

By Charles Brockden Brown or Gouverneur Morris.

B.A.L. 1511; not attr. S. 8127. Reprint of no. 07-02 with seven pages added entitled "(William) Cobbett against himself". The second edition is stated on the title page to be by Morris.

08-11   The case of Baptis Irvine, in a matter of contempt of court.
         With an appendix, by a Gentleman of the Bar. From the
         Reporter's short-hand notes . . . Baltimore . . . 1808 . . . 8vo.
         57, 48p.

         The "Gentleman of the Bar" was Theodorick Bland. The
         Reporter was George Bourne.

         Bland is identified in Eberstadt Cat. 168 #47; not identi-
         fied Bristol 641; S. 35112; Shaw 14648. The appendix is
         entitled "An essay on constructive contempt of Court . . ."
         Shaw 14959.

08-12   The citizens of Knox County, Tennessee . . . (Knoxville, 1808).

         By James Trimble.

         Shaw 50892.

08-13   Communications on the next election for president . . . and on
         the late measures of the federal administration . . . By a
         citizen of New York . . . 1808. 8vo. 40p.

         By Edmond C. E. Genet.

         S. 26928(70p.); Cronin & Wise, Madison 139; CHA 4514 3:4;
         Shaw 15093. S. 15007 not attr.

08-14   Considerations on the Embargo Laws. (Boston, 1808). 8vo.
         16p.

         By Daniel Webster.

         S. 102257; Johnston p. 37; Wise & Cronin 778; Shaw
         16688; D.A.B. 19:586; Kress B5468; CHA 5170 3:5. S.
         15983 not attr.

08-15   Considerations on the jurisprudence of the State of Pennsylvania
         . . . Philadelphia 1808. 8vo. 10p.

         By Hugh Henry Brackenridge?

         Jeff. 3368; B.A.L. 1318; Shaw 14570. S. 60008 not attr.

08-16   Economy. Thoughts on a Plan of economy (suited to the crisis of 1808) for the United States of America. Sgd, S. B. (n.p. 1808). 8vo. 8p. incl. tables.

By Samuel Blodget, Jr.

S. 5957; Shaw 14540; Kress B5614 (see also Kress B5341).

08-17   The embargo, a song composed . . . at Dover July 4th, 1808 . . . Dover Landing (N.H. 1808). Broadside.

By Henry Mellen.

Shaw 15579.

08-18   The embargo, or sketches of the times; A satire. By a youth of thirteen. Boston . . . 1808. 12mo. 12p.

By William Cullen Bryant.

S. 22409; B.A.L. 1582; Weg. 890; Cush. 1 p. 313; Johnston p. 35.

08-19   An essay on descents . . . (New Haven? 1808?). 24p.

By William Hillhouse.

Shaw 15232; STE 45886, suggests 1790. See no. 08-38.

08-20   Essays, on the legal import of the term "heirs" . . . (New Haven? 1808?).

By William Hillhouse.

Shaw 15233. See preceding entry.

08-21   Examen des Droits des Etats-Unis et des pretentions de Mr. Edouard Livingston sur la Batture . . . Nouvelle-Orléans . . . 1808. 4to. 50p. 3 plans.

By Jean Baptiste Simon Thierry.

Jeff. 3477; Shaw 16306; S. 95344. See next entry.

08-22   Examination of the claim of the United States, and of the pretentions of Edward Livingston, Esq. to the Batture . . . New-Orleans . . . 1808. 4to. 52p. 3 plans.

By Jean Baptiste Simon Thierry.

Jeff. 3478; Shaw 16307; S. 95345. Signed "Thierry."

08-23   An examination of the conduct of Great Britain respecting
        neutrals . . . second edition . . . Boston 1808. 8vo. 72p.

        By Tench Coxe.

        Kress B5329; Shaw 14792; S. 17297. S. 43708 attr. to
        James Madison. For first edition see no. 07-10.

08-24   A faithful picture of the political situation of New Orleans . . .
        Boston, reprinted . . . 1808. 8vo. (5)6-48p.

        By James Workman?

        S. 105480+; CHA 3153 3:3. For first edition see no. 07-
        12. S. 53325; Shaw 14981; Tompk. Burr 46 not attr.

08-25   Hints to both parties . . . orders in council . . . London . . .
        1808. 8vo. (5)vi,95p.; also New York . . . 1808. 8vo. 92,
        (60)p.

        By Joseph Marryat?

        Kress B5396 (London), 5374 (New York not attr.); not attr.
        S. 31981 or Shaw 15238.

08-26   The history of . . . Miranda's attempt to effect a revolution in
        South America . . . Boston, 1808. By an officer under that
        general. 12mo. (12)300p.

        By James Biggs.

        Jeff. 4160 (171 leaves); S. 5333; Howes B442; Cush. 1 p.
        116; Shaw 14515. In Cush. 1 p. 209, S. 9117 and Halk. 3p.
        66 attribution is to Henry Adams Bullard.

08-27   The honest politician . . . to the President . . . Baltimore . . .
        1808. 8vo. viii(1)4-65p. l.

        By Luther Martin?

        Johnston p. 36; CHA 9472 2:7 has name handwritten;
        Bristol 639 suggests Martin; not attr. S. 32777; Wise &
        Cronin 502; Shaw 15262.

08-28   Interesting correspondence . . . Governour Sullivan and Col.
         Pickering . . . Boston . . . 1808. 8vo. 32p. Has "charges
         made against him" in title. Another issue and also second
         edition has "charges and insinuations made". Newburyport
         edition has "charges made".

         By Timothy Pickering.

         S. 93500+, 62650. Shaw 15307-09 not attr. Shaw 16267-9
         under James Sullivan.

08-29   A letter addressed to the Hon. James Madison, Secretary of
         State . . . 1808 . . . (Philadelphia). 8vo. (2)35p. Also 35p.

         By Rufus King?

         Shaw 15417; S. 40259 not attr. Compiler has copy noted
         in early hand: "By Hon. Rufus King".

08-30   A letter, on the approaching election of a president of the
         United States . . . by a native of Charleston . . . Charleston
         1808. 8vo. 27p.

         By William Loughton Smith?

         S. 87863; Turnbull p. 445; CHA 12557 1:4. Not attr. in
         Jeff. 3372; Shaw 15419; Cronin & Wise, Madison 146; S.
         40364+?, 40365, 40434; not in Rogers.

08-31   Letter to the Electors of President and Vice President of the
         United States. By a Citizen of New York. New York . . .
         1808. 8vo. 22p.

         By Edmond Charles Genet.

         S. 26931; Wise & Cronin 462; Cush. 1 p. 59; Shaw 15094;
         not attr. S. 40471.

08-32   A letter to the President of the United States, touching the
         prosecutions, under his patronage . . . Circuit Court . . .
         Connecticut . . . By Hampden . . . New-Haven . . . 1808.
         8vo. 28p.

         By David Daggett or Noah Webster, Jr.?

         Purcell p. 437 attr. to Webster; not Skeel; no attribution

in Tompk. Jeff. 199; S. 30125; Shaw 15422. Theodore
Dwight, "The Character of Thomas Jefferson . . ." Boston,
1839, pp. 309, 310, states that the work "was understood
at the time to have been written by . . . counsel in the
prosecutions". Daggett was chief defense counsel.

08-33   Memoirs of the northern kingdom . . . six letters . . . (Boston,
        1808). 8vo. 48p.

        By William Jenks.

        S. 36033; Shaw 15319; Johnston p. 36; D.A.B. 10:54;
        Morison 537.

08-34   The militia laws of this Commonwealth . . . Richmond . . .
        1808. 8vo. 55p.

        By William Waller Hening.

        D.A.B. 8:537. Shaw 16643 not attr.

08-35   Observations on the American treaty, in eleven letters . . .
        London, 1808. Sgd, Decius. 8vo. (7),75,(1)p.

        By Thomas Peregrine Courtenay.

        S. 17183; Kress B5327; Cush. 1 p. 79; Halk. 4 p. 218. His
        "additional observations" London 1808 bear his name. S.
        17184.

08-36   A political sermon, addressed to the electors of Middlesex.
        (1808). 8vo. 39p.

        By Samuel P. P. Fay.

        Brin. 4953, Vol. I. S. 63805; Shaw 15968 not attr.

08-37   The present state of our country considered, in an address to
        the Freemen of Vermont, by a farmer of Windham County.
        (1808). 31p.

        By John Phelps.

        McCorison 1022; Shaw 15905; not attr. S. 99200.

08-38   Reading No. 1 or Considerations on the Statute of Distributions

... New-Haven ... 1808. 8vo. 32p.

By William Hillhouse.

Not listed S. Shaw 15234. Reprints plaintiff's brief in Hillhouse vs. Chester. 3 Day (Conn.) Rep. 166 (1808), in which
Hillhouse was plaintiff and also plaintiff's counsel (he lost).
David Daggett was also for plaintiff, but the "I" at the con-
clusion of the brief indicates Hillhouse as author. See also
nos. 08-19, 20.

08-39   Reasons offered ... in favor of the removal of the seat of
        Government ... to Philadelphia ... (Washington City,
        1808). 8p.

        By James Sloan.

        Shaw 16198; CHA 20045 1:4.

08-40   Remarks and criticisms on ... John Quincy Adam's letter to
        ... Harrison Gray Otis. Boston ... 1808. 8vo. 1p., l., 62p.

        By William Coleman.

        S. 14313; Brin. 4817, 4953; Cronin & Wise, J. Q. Adams
        228; Shaw 14725; CHA 4730 3:2.

08-41   Remarks on Mr. Gaston's Address to the freemen of the
        Counties of Wayne ... (Newbern, N.C. 1808), Signed, A
        Republican. 8vo. 44p.

        By   Woods.

        S. 105118; Cronin & Wise, Madison 203; Shaw 16762. See
        no. 08-03.

08-42   Report, in part, of the Committee appointed ... President's
        Message ... Foreign Relations ... Washington City. 1808.
        8vo. 16p.

        By Albert Gallatin.

        Bemis 143; Raymond Walters, Jr. "Albert Gallatin", p. 204;
        not attr. Shaw 16545; S. 69736.

08-43   A report on the present alarming state of national affairs ...

(Schenectady, 1808). 15p.

By Alexander Kelly?

Shaw 15348, 15003.

08-44   Sermon. The question of war with Great Britain examined . . .
        Boston . . . 1808. 8vo. 14p.

By Joseph Dana or Joseph McKean.

S. 18435; Sibley 14:588n, 590 attr. to Dana. S. 43376,
79285; Shaw 15472 attr. to McKean.

08-45   Some remarks and extracts, in reply to Mr. Pickering's letter
        . . . Embargo. Caption title. New Haven, one issue undated
        (1808); one issue dated 1808. 8vo. 23(1)p.

By Abraham Bishop.

Dex. 4 p. 22; Shaw 14528. S. 86732 not attr.

08-46   Thoughts upon the conduct of our administration . . . Great
        Britain and France . . . the Chesapeake. By a Friend to
        Peace. Boston 1808. 8vo. 28p.

By John Lowell.

S. 42462+, 95729+; Tompk. Jeff. 210; Kress B5391; CHA
4291 1:2; Howes L535; not attr. in S. 12490.

08-47   To the public. Various statements . . . having been made . . .
        against the governor . . . 1808. Natchez. Broadside.

By Robert Williams.

McMurtrie 48; Shaw 16743.

08-48   Walter Kennedy: an interesting American tale . . . London . . .
        1808. 16mo., 2p., l., (1)iv-vii, 192p.

By John Davis.

CHA 5824 2:6; S. 101204; including Kaskaskia Indian
vocabulary. See no. 05-32.

08-49   The whole truth. To the freemen of New-England. (Boston

1808). Signed, Hancock. 8vo. 38p.; also 12mo. 35p.

By Jonathan Russell.

S. 74359, 103849; Jeff. 3455; CHA 6629 3:3,4; Cush. 2 p. 72; Shaw 16116, 16117; not attr. S. 30196.

1809

09-01 Address of "The United Whig Club" to their fellow Republicans of the State of New York. New York. 1809. 8vo.

By Robert Macomb.

S. 43614; Cushing, "Anonyms", p. 10; NYHS 69; cited Shaw 17965. See Shaw 19080.

09-02 An address to the Congress of the United States, . . . restrictions upon foreign commerce . . . Philadelphia . . . 1809. 8vo. (8), 94,(1)p.

By Charles Brockden Brown.

S. 8456; Jeff. 3464; B.A.L. 1513; Kress B5487; Howes B830; Shaw 17089; S. has 97 pages.

09-03 Address to the people of the Commonwealth of Massachusetts. Boston . . . 1809. 8vo. 24p. (in five versions—one reads "red and concurred"; another uses black letter, &c.); also 15p.

By Harrison Gray Otis?

Shaw 18309; in Shaw 17030 attr. to Timothy Bigelow; not attr. Shaw 18021-24. Otis was President of the Senate, where the Address originated. Morison 308: "he may be presumed to have had much to do with this". Bigelow was House Speaker.

09-04 An address to the people of the county of Hampshire . . . Northampton (Mass.) . . . 1809. 8vo. 20p.

By Charles Porter Phelps?

Noted on compiler's copy as "by your friend C. Porter
Phelps Esq." Phelps is named as one of the committee who
prepared the address. Not attr. Shaw 16808.

09-05   An address to the people of New England ... by Algernon
Sidney (n.p. 1809). 12mo. 36p.; Albany, 1809, 32p.;
Kingston, 38p.; (Northampton) 1809, 32p.; Philadelphia
... 1809. 32p.; Portsmouth 1809. 36p.; Trenton ...
1809. 38p.; n.p.35p.

By Gideon Granger.

Shaw 17651-17658; Howes G300; S. 28281, 80854;
CHA 6627 2:5-7, 8367 1:7; Kress B5508,09. See no. 08-
05.

09-06   American candour, in a tract ... entitled an analysis of the late
correspondence ... London ... 1809. 8vo. (4)106p.

By John Lowell.

Kress B5529. S. 1068 not attr. Reprint of no. 09-08.

09-07   American principles. A review of works of Fisher Ames ...
Boston ... 1809. 8vo. 56p.

By John Quincy Adams.

S. 273; Brin. 4953; Cronin & Wise, J. Q. Adams 12;
Shaw 16797.

09-08   Analysis of the late correspondence between our administration
and Great Britain & France ... Boston (1809). 8vo. 52p.;
New York. 8vo. iv(1)6-56p.

By John Lowell.

S. 42443; CHA 13041 2:7; Brin. 4886; Shaw 17933,
17934; Shaw 15457 has (1808) but this is very unlikely.

09-09   Biographical memoirs of the illustrious General George Washington ... New Haven ... 1809. 18mo. 144p., front.

By John Corry.

S. 101778; Baker 74. See no. 08-09. Shaw 17273 has

Thomas Condie, who had a work with almost the same title —see no. 00-07.

09-10   Biographical sketch of the character of Governor Trumbull. (Hartford, 1809). 8vo. 13p. Caption title.

By John Trumbull.

S. 97205; Dex. 3:256. Shaw 17046 not attr. Also appears as appendix to Ely, Zebulon: Sermon ... S. 22392; Shaw 17437.

09-11   Cases and queries submitted to every citizen ... especially the Members of the Administration ... New York 1809. 8vo. 24p.

By Egbert Benson.

S. 4742, 11323; Kress B5484; D.A.B. 2:204. Shaw 17164 not attr.

09-12   Considerations on the abolition of the common law in the United States ... Philadelphia ... 1809. v(1)8-71p.

By Joseph Hopkinson.

Shaw 17775; attr. in L.C. and Yale catalogues; S. 15958 not attr.

09-13   A cursory sketch of the motives ... of the Party ... present crisis ... Philadelphia. 1809. 8vo. 38p.

By Henry Lee.

S. 39740; Johnston p. 37; Wise & Cronin 552; Shaw 17901.

09-14   Examination of the judgment ... Jean Gravier and the City of New Orleans ... Washington ... 1809 ... 8vo. 19p.

By Louis C. E. Moreau de Lislet.

Jeff. 3490; Shaw 18124. S. 28363 not attr. See no. 07-09 for French original.

09-15   The history ... Miranda's attempt to effect a revolution in South America ... second edition. Boston 1809. xi(1) 300p.; London 1809. 8vo. xv(1)312p.

By James Biggs.

S. 5333,34; CHA 9356 3:2; Shaw 17031. See no. 08-26.

09-16   Interesting Political Discussion. The diplomatick policy of Mr. Madison unveiled (caption). By a Bostonian. (Boston, 1809?). 8vo. 55p.

By John Lowell.

Shaw 17936; Howes L530; Cronin & Wise, Madison 149, 150. S. 42451 suggests 1812.

09-17   A memoir on the subject of a navigation act . . . manufactory of boats . . . Philadelphia . . . 1809. 16p.

By Tench Coxe?

Kress B5545. Shaw 18065 not attr. The Kress copy has ms. note on title page: "T. Coxe".

09-18   Memoirs of Gen. George Washington . . . fourth edition . . . Philadelphia . . . 1809. 24mo. 143p.

By Thomas Condie.

Shaw 17274; S. 101851.

09-19   Memoirs of the Hon. Thomas Jefferson . . . (New York) 1809. 2 vols. 8vo. iv,404; (2)434p.

By Stephen C. Carpenter.

S. 11004; Swem 792; Howes C164; Shaw 17154; D.A.B. 3:513.

09-20   Men and measures, from 1774 to 1809 . . . By a Native American . . . Washington . . . 1809. 12mo. 24p.

By James Jones Wilmer.

Jeff. 3386; Shaw 19246; S. 104569 has "Men and manners".

09-21   New-Haven, a Poem . . . with Historical . . . notes . . . by Selim . . . New York . . . 1809. 12mo. 34p.

By Samuel Woodworth.

S. 105189; Weg. 1215; D.A.B. 20:512; Shaw 19264.

09-22   Observations on a letter from Noah Webster . . . by an old-
         fashioned clergyman . . . New Haven . . . 1809 . . . 8vo. 24p.

         By John Bowden.

         Shaw 17073; Skeel 706 n.3; not mentioned D.A.B. 2:491;
         not attr. S. 56489.

09-23   Pills, poetical, political and philosophical . . . By Peter Pepper
         Box . . . Philadelphia . . . 1809. 12mo. (20)136p.

         By Thomas Green Fessenden.

         S. 62855; Brin. 8314; Weg. 960; Wise & Cronin 445; Shaw
         17506. See Porter G. Perrin, Thomas Green Fessenden, Uni-
         versity of Maine studies second series, no. 4 (1925), p. 130
         et seq.

09-24   A poetical picture of America . . . a residence of several years
         . . . in Virginia . . . 1799 to 1807 . . . By a lady . . . London.
         1809. 16mo., 7p., l., 177p; or (14), 177p.

         By Anne Ritson.

         CHA 25048 1:5; S. 63648, 71587+; Clark 2:118.

09-25   Proofs of the corruption of Gen. James Wilkinson and of his
         connexion with Aaron Burr . . . by Daniel Clark . . . Phila-
         delphia . . . 1809. 8vo. (2)150,199p.

         By Daniel Coxe, Edward Livingston, and others.

         Thomas R. Hay and M. R. Werner, The Admirable Trumpeter,
         a biography of General James Wilkinson, p. 299; from copy
         furnished by Clark. Shaw 17221, Clark.

09-26   Reflections upon the Administration of Justice in Pennsylvania.
         By a citizen . . . Philadelphia . . . 1809. 8vo. 66p.

         By Richard Rush?

         Compiler has copy endorsed "R^d Rush", from C. L. Robin-
         son cat. no. 92. Not attr. in S. 60446; Shaw 18483.

09-27   Remarks on the Hon. John Q. Adams' review of Mr. Ames's
Works ... Boston ... 1809. 8vo. (3)iv,v(2)8-50p.

By John Lowell.

S. 42459; Brin. 4953; Cronin & Wise, J. Q. Adams 265;
Shaw 17937. S. 43375; Shaw 17957 attr. to Joseph
McKean.

09-28   Reply to Mr. Duponceau (New Orleans, 1809). 8vo. 68p.

By Jean Baptiste Simon Thierry.

Jeff. 3491; S. 95346; Shaw 18748; signed "Thierry"
on page 34.

09-29   Reponse à Mr. Du Ponceau (New Orleans, 1809). 8vo. 67p.

By Jean Baptiste Simon Thierry.

S. 95347; Shaw 18749. See preceding entry.

09-30   Supplement to the late analysis ... correspondence ... our
Cabinet and ... France and G. Britain. (Boston, 1809).
8vo. 28p.; also New York iv(1)6-56p.

By John Lowell.

Kress B5531,32; Shaw 17938; S. 42444 (1808 is error);
S. 93806+; Brin. 4886. See no. 09-08 for the "Analysis".

09-31   Things as they are; or, Federalism turned inside out!! ...
Baltimore ... (1809). 8vo. 75p.

By Hezekiah Niles.

S. 55313; Johnston 37; Jeff. 3384; CHA 21335 3:6;
Bristol 776; Wise & Cronin 616; Shaw 18257.

09-32   A tour through part of Virginia, in the summer of 1808 ...
New York ... 1809. 8vo. 31p.

By John Edwards Caldwell.

Clark, ed. 2:139; Howes C23; CHA 3258 1:2. S. 9917,
96334+ has T. Caldwell; S. 100532+ favors Samuel L.
Mitchill; Howes M704 has Mitchill and other Caldwells.

See 1951 reprint edited by William M. E. Rachal, Richmond, The Dietz Press.

09-33   A view of the political situation of the province of Upper Canada ... London ... 1809. 8vo. (6)vii-xi(1)79p.

By John Mills Jackson.

S. 35438; Kress B5519.

09-34   The whole truth. An address to the freemen of . . . New England ... Fredericktown ... 1809. 8vo. 66p.; Charles-town (W. Va.) 1809. 8vo. 31p.

By Jonathan Russell.

Shaw 18552; Streeter 1106 (Charles-town); not attr. S. 103850. See no. 08-49.

09-35   The whole truth; or, the Essex Junto exposed . . . by Hancock ... New York. (1809). 8vo. 19p.; Troy 1809. 8vo. 47p.

By Jonathan Russell.

S. 103851,52; Shaw 18553,54. See preceding entry.

1810

10-01   An address to the independent citizens of Massachusetts . . . Jefferson & Madison administrations. Worcester . . . 1810. 8vo. 23p.

By John Lowell.

Abridgement by an unknown of "The New England patriot . . .", no. 10-23. Shaw 19309 not attr.

10-02   An address to the independent electors of the State of New York ... Albany (1810). 8vo. 16p.

By DeWitt Clinton?

See Shaw 19790; Hammond 282; not attr. in S. 53504;

Shaw 19310.

10-03   Appeal to the people . . . rejection of the British Minister . . .
        New York . . . 1810. 8vo. xiii, 123p.

        By William Coleman.

        S. 14310; Shaw 19797; D.A.B. 4:295; CHA 1191 2:4.

10-04   The bank torpedo; or bank notes proved to be a robbery on the
        public . . . by a friend to common honesty . . . New York
        . . . 1810. 59p.

        By Benjamin Davies.

        Kress B5639; S. 18749; Shaw 19920.

10-05   Biographical Memoirs of the illustrious General George Washing-
        ton . . . N. Haven . . . 1810. 18mo. 144p. front; also Wil-
        mington . . . 1810. 18mo. 108p.

        By John Corry.

        S. 16916, 101778; CHA 5294 1:2; Shaw 19869, 19870;
        Baker 80. Reprint of no. 09-09.

10-06   A brief view of the policy and resources of the United States
        . . . Philadelphia . . . 1810. 8vo. (5)iv-viii,3-133p.; also
        London viii,135p.

        By Robert Hare.

        S. 30369; Kress B5665; CHA 2858 2:7; Shaw 20282. In
        answer to no. 10-17.

10-07   The diplomatic policy of Mr. Madison unveiled . . . By a
        Bostonian . . . London . . . 1810. 8vo. 80p.

        By John Lowell.

        S. 42446; CHA 6148 2:1. See next entry.

10-08   The diplomatick policy of Mr. Madison unveiled . . . (Boston,
        1810). 8vo. 52p.

        By John Lowell.

Howes L530; Shaw 20598; Kress B5533 (1809). See no. 09-16.

10-09   Economica . . . statistical manual . . . additions to 1810 . . . Washington . . . 1810. 8vo. (8)202,xiv,8p.

By Samuel Blodget, Jr.

S. 5956; Howes B537; Shaw 19579. See no. 06-11.

10-10   England and France; or, the contrast . . . London . . . 1810. 12mo. (3)iv(1)47(1)p.

By Robert Walsh.

Extracted from no. 10-17; S. 22589 not attr.

10-11   An essay on Federalism. (Frankfort, Ky.? 1810). Caption title. 64p.

By Joseph H. Daveiss.

A.I.I. 5:351; Shaw 19918; Howes D79.

10-12   An essay on the establishment of a chancery jurisdiction in Massachusetts. Boston (1810). 8vo. 90p.

By Erastus Worthington.

S. 22957, 105499+; Shaw 22104; Ap. Cyc. 6:617.

10-13   A general course of preparatory study for the duties of the bar . . . New York, 1810. 12mo. 35p.

By John Anthon.

NYHS 13. Shaw 20195 not attr.

10-14   History of the discovery of America . . . by the Rev. James Steward, D.D. . . . Brooklyn (1810?). 8vo. v(2)8-176p.

By Henry Trumbull.

CHA 21667 1:3; S. 97192. Other editions have name in copyright or on title page. Shaw 20343, 21529-31.

10-15   The history of . . . Miranda's attempt to effect a revolution in South America . . . Boston . . . 1810 . . . 8vo. xi,312p.

By James Biggs.

S. 5333; Shaw 19553; CHA 2238 2:7. See no. 09-15.

10-16 Inchiquin, the Jesuit's Letters . . . New York . . . 1810. 8vo. v,165p.

By Charles J. Ingersoll.

S. 34732; Brin. 4866; Shaw 20436; CHA 9819 1:3.

10-17 A letter on the genius and dispositions of the French Government . . . by an American recently returned from Europe. Baltimore 1810. 8vo. iv,253p. (two issues); Philadelphia 1810 8vo. iv,253p.; second edition, Boston 1810 8vo. (5)6-114(2)p.; third (-tenth, twelfth) editions, London 1810 iv,252p.

By Robert Walsh.

Bristol 901; S. 101165; Kress B5762-71; Shaw 21934-36.

10-18 A Letter to the Honorable John Randolph. By Numa. (Caption, dated February 21, 1810). 8vo. 38(1)p.

By John B. Colvin.

Jeff. 3376; not attr. in S. 67849; Shaw 20940.

10-19 Letters of Marcus and Philo-Cato . . . (New York) . . . 1810. 8vo. iv,86p.

By William Peter Van Ness (Marcus) and Matthew L. Davis (Philo-Cato).

S. 18863, 98531+; Tompk. Burr 39; Shaw 19929; CHA 4638 1:4; Hammond 227 (Davis). See no. 06-20.

10-20 Lines on duelling . . . originally published in the Visitor . . . (Richmond, 1810). (7)8-23p. errata leaf.

By Louis H. Girardin.

Davis pp. 265, 467 n. 23; Shaw 51009; Weg. 973.

10-21 Mémoire sur la conduite de la France et de L'Angleterre à l'égard des nuitres. Paris . . . 1810. (4)243p.

By Charles Louis Lesur?

Bookseller's attribution; S. 47533 not attr.

10-22   The new crisis . . . by an old whig . . . New York . . . 1810. 8vo.
         96p.

By James Cheetham.

S. 12382 (95p.); Shaw 19762; CHA 4278 2:3; not attr.
S. 52583.

10-23   The New England patriot . . . comparison . . . of the Washington
         and Jefferson administrations . . . Boston . . . 1810. 8vo.
         (2)148(12)p.

By John Lowell.

S. 42453; Dumbauld p. 257; Howes L532; Shaw 20600.

10-24   Observations on canal navigation. (1810). 8vo. 15p.

By Thomas Eddy?

Shaw 20025; NYHS 41 ("with a plate").

10-25   Paragraphs on banks . . . Philadelphia . . . 1810. 8vo. vi(1)4-
         73p.

By Erick Bollman.

Kress B5615; Shaw 19584; not attr. in S. 58511, but see
S. 6237 for 1811 edition under his name.

10-26   The passage of the president's message, which relates to the
         forcible occupation of West Florida . . . signed, Verus.
         (1810?). 8vo. 20p. No t.p.

By Luis de Onis?

CHA 7203 2:1; S. 99315; Shaw 20955; Streeter 1534.
Erratum slip pasted on p. 20.

10-27   Political queries and statements. Addressed to candid men . . .
         n.p. (1810). 8vo. 15p.

By Abijah Bigelow.

S. 5271; Shaw 19552.

10-28   Reflections upon the late correspondence . . . Secretary Smith
and Francis James Jackson . . . Baltimore . . . 1810. 8vo.
(3)4-97p.

By Alexander C. Hanson.

Bristol 856; S. 30257; Shaw 20278; CHA 8905 2:5.

10-29   Remarks on the documents accompanying the late message of
President Madison . . . (n.p., 1810). 8vo. 48p.

By Theodore Dwight.

S. 21533; Shaw 20016.

10-30   A Sketch of the life and character . . . George Washington . . .
Palmer . . . (1810?). 18mo. 64p.

By Ezekiel Terry.

S. 94893; Howes T107; Shaw 21475.

10-31   Ten hints addressed to wise men . . . dismission of Mr. Jackson,
the British minister . . . (Boston 1810). 8vo. 115p. Caption
title.

By John Lowell?

S. 42449; Shaw 17940; Kress B5534 (1809); S. 94678
(1810) notes an attribution to Benjamin Vaughan; Shaw
21889, Vaughan. The dismission occurred November 8,
1809.

10-32   A tour through part of Virginia, in the summer of 1808 . . . also
some account of the Azores . . . Belfast 1810. 12mo. 63p.

By John Edwards Caldwell.

See no. 09-32. S. 9917, 100533 (where Samuel L. Mitchill
is finally favored); Kress B5753 (various).

10-33   A true account of the defalcation of the Hillsborough Bank . . .
Concord . . . (1810?). 8vo. 16p.

By Eli Brown.

Turner p. 195n.; not attr. S. 31914; Shaw 22408 (1811).

10-34   Washington und die Nordamerikanische Revolution . . . Giessen
        . . . 1810. 12mo. 280p.(?).

By Josias Ludwig Gosch.

S. 42171, 101898+; Baker 82. See no. 07-38.

INDEX OF WORKS WITH DATES ASCRIBED

AUTHOR INDEX

Adams, John. 1735-1826,   05-13
   Second President.
Adams, John Quincy. 1767-1848.   92-20, 93-03, 09-07
   Minister 1794-1801; U.S. Senator 1803-1808;
   Sixth President.
Addison, Alexander. 1759-1807.   98-33
   Federalist Judge, Pa., removed 1803.
Allen, Ira. 1751-1814.   97-62
   Soldier, author, of Vermont.
Allen, Richard. 1760-1831.   94-21
   Methodist minister, Philadelphia.
Allen, William. 1770-1843?   92-12
   Englishman.
Allison, Patrick. 1740-1802.   93-05
   Maryland clergyman.
Almon, John. 1737-1804.   97-08
   English bookseller, author and editor.
Alsop, Richard. 1761-1815.   90-24, 90-28, 95-04, 99-36, 03-33, 07-07
   Connecticut author.
Alston, Joseph. 1778-1816.   07-27
   So. Carolina legislature, 1802-12. Husband of
   Theodosia Burr.
Ames, Fisher. 1758-1808.   04-46
   Congressman from Mass., 1789-1797.
Anderson, Charles.   01-23
   Of Wilmington, Del.
Anthon, John. 1784-1863.   10-13
   Lawyer of New York City.
Appleton, John S.   -1824,   08-08
   Of Salem, Massachusetts, bookseller.
Arden, Thomas S.   .   05-09
   Bookseller of New York City.
Armstrong, John. 1758-1843.   97-28, 98-67, 03-18, 06-13
   Born Pa. Senator from N.Y., 1800-02;
   1803-04; Minister France 1804-1810.

Benson, Egbert. 1746-1833. 09-11
  Congressman from N.Y. 1789-93; Judge.
Bentley, William. 1759-1819. 99-22, 02-27
  Massachusetts clergyman; diarist.
Beresford, Richard. 1755-1803. 93-28, 97-59
  Member Continental Congress. Lawyer,
  Charleston, S.C.
Beresford, William. 89-23
  English author.
Berquin-Duvallon, F. 03-37, 06-40
  French author, of St. Domingue.
Biddle, Owen. 90-20
  Of Philadelphia.
Bidwell, Barnabas. 1763-1833. 96-75, 00-28, 04-07, 05-04
  Senator from Mass. 1801-05; Representative
  1806-07; Mass. Attorney General 1807-10.
Bigelow, Abijah. 10-27
Bigelow, Timothy. 1767-1821. 09-03
  Lawyer, Mass. legislature, Hartford Convention.
Biggs, James. 08-26, 09-15, 10-15
  Of Massachusetts; friend of de Miranda.
Bingham, William. 1752-1804. 93-09
  Senator from Pennsylvania, 1795-1801.
Binns, John. 1772-1860. 07-28
  Publisher, Alderman, Philadelphia.
Bird, Henry Merrtins. 94-36
  English merchant.
Bishop, Abraham. 1763-1844. 91-21, 01-20, 02-07, 04-50, 08-45
  New Haven Court Clerk and Collector.
Bland, Theodorick. 08-11
  Maryland Chancellor.
Blodget, Samuel (Sr.). 1724-1807. 99-46, 06-37
  Inventor, canal builder, of Mass.
Blodget, Samuel, Jr. 1757-1814. 01-22, 06-11, 06-37, 08-16, 10-09
  Architect, economist of Washington, D.C.
Blodget, William. 05-14
  Of Pennsylvania, Connecticut.
Blyth, Stephen C. -1840. 06-15
  Physician, of Salem, Mass.
Boileau, Nathaniel B. 1763-18-. 05-26
  Pennsylvania legislature 1792-1802; 1803-.

Brown, James.   00-09
   English clergyman.
Brown, John.   05-33, 07-06
   Englishman, of Yarmouth.
Brown, William. 1764-1803.   00-11
   Federalist lawyer of Hartford, Connecticut.
Bruce, David.   01-14
   Pennsylvanian, of Scottish origin.
Bruce, John. 1745-1826.   96-68
   Scottish historian.
Bryan, Captain.   91-06
Bryan, Samuel.   00-55
   Pennsylvania official.
Bryant, William Cullen. 1794-1878.   08-18
   Author.
Bullard, Henry Adams. 1788-1851.   08-26
   Lawyer, Louisiana Judge.
Burges, James Bland. 1752-1824.   90-15
   English Under-Secretary of State.
Burn, A.   92-27
   English Major-General.
Burr, Aaron. 1756-1836.   04-09
   Soldier, U.S. Senator 1791-97; Vice President
   1801-05.
Burwell, William B. 1780(?)-1821.   07-32
   Congressman from Va. 1806-1821.

Caldwell, Charles. 1772-1853.   99-18, 00-19, 00-20, 02-32
   Physician, Philadelphia.
Caldwell, John E. 1769-1819.   09-32, 10-32
   Merchant, of Philadelphia, N.Y.
Callender, James Thomson. 1758-1803.   94-27, 95-39, 95-45, 96-17,
   Political writer Philadelphia,   97-03, 97-25, 00-40, 01-16, 02-19
   Richmond, 1793-1803.
Camac, Turner.   05-14
Campe, Joachim H. Von. 1746-1818.   03-36
   German educator, writer.
Carey, James.   96-29, 96-44, 97-06, 98-31, 98-40, 98-46, 99-10
   Publisher Va., S.C., Ga., N.C. and Pa.   99-48
Carey, Mathew. 1760-1839. 90-13, 94-33, 95-03, 95-19, 96-04, 96-17
   Publisher and author of Philadelphia   98-31, 99-45

Carlisle, Frederick Howard, Earl of. 1748-1825.   98-69
    English poet, essayist.
Carondelet, Baron de. 1748-1807.   94-04
    Spanish Governor La. and West Fla. 1791-97.
Carpenter, Stephen C.   -1820.   09-19
    Author, Charleston, S.C.
Carr, Matthew. 1750-1820.   00-53
    Minister, Philadelphia.
Carroll, Daniel.   -1829.   02-15
    Of Md., son of Daniel the Signer.
Carroll, James.   97-53
Carroll, John. 1735-1817.   96-03
    Catholic archbishop of Maryland.
Chandler, Samuel.   89-18
    Of Georgia.
Chassanis, Pierre.   92-11
    Frenchman.
Chasseboeuf, Constantin, Comte de Volney. 1757-1820.   95-10
    French traveller in U.S.
Chauvet, David.   98-12, 98-35
    Swiss-American.
Cheetham, James. 1772-1810.   00-06, 00-32, 01-18, 02-04, 02-05,
    Journalist, author,   02-23, 02-33, 03-17, 06-16, 06-29, 10-22
    of N.Y.
Chester, Leonard. 1750-1803.   02-14
    Of Wethersfield, Conn.
Cheves, Langdon. 1776-1857.   08-07
    So. Carolina legislature 1802-09.
Childs, Thomas.   00-07
Chipman, Samuel, Jr. fl. 1798.   99-35
    Vermont publisher.
Church, Edward, Jr. 1779-1845.   89-02
    Merchant, writer, of Northampton, Mass.
Clay, Matthew. 1754-1815.   97-37
    Congressman from Va. 1795-1813.
Clerk, John. 1728-1812.   99-44
    Scottish naval tactician, etcher.
Cliffton, William. 1772-1799.   96-26, 96-77
    Poet, of Philadelphia.
Clinton, DeWitt. 1769-1828.   00-63, 04-14, 10-02
    N.Y. legislature 1797-1802; Mayor N.Y.;
    Pres. candidate 1812.

Coxe, Tench. 1755-1824.   89-08, 91-07, 92-06, 92-25, 93-27, 96-23,
    Ass't. Sec'y. Treas.   99-05, 99-06, 00-56, 04-24, 06-39, 07-10,
    1789-92; Comm. of Revenue 1792-97;   08-23, 09-17
    Purveyor of Supplies.
Crafton, William Bell.   92-03, 92-30
    English author.
Cranch, William. 1769-1855.   01-09
    Jurist; Washington judge, 1801-55.
Crawford, Charles. 1752-   93-24
    Poet, essayist, of Philadelphia?
Crevecoeur, Michel G. J. de (John Hector St. John).   93-18, 98-36,
    1731-1813. French traveller, Consul at N.Y. 1783.   01-26
Currie, James. 1756-1805.   93-16
    Merchant, physician, of Liverpool.
Cutler, Manasseh. 1742-1823.   89-04
    Revolutionary hero, lawyer, clergyman, physician,
    scientist, Congressman from Mass. 1801-05.

Daggett, David. 1764-1851.   00-58, 03-14, 04-19, 05-31, 08-32,
    Lawyer, Conn. legislature 1791-1813.   08-38
Dallas, Alexander James. 1759-1817.   90-17, 93-06, 95-19, 95-26,
    Sec'y., Pa. 1791-1801; U.S. Att'y., Pa.   02-01, 05-01
    1801-14; Sec'y. Treas. 1814-16.
Dana, Joseph. 1742-1827.   08-44
    Clergyman, Massachusetts.
Dana, Samuel W. 1760-1830.   00-24, 02-30
    Congressman from Conn. 1797-1810;
    Senator 1810-21.
Daveiss, Joseph Hamilton. 1774-1811.   10-11
    Lawyer; U.S. Attorney for Kentucky.
Davies, Benjamin. fl. 1774-1810.   96-77, 10-04
    Publisher, bookseller, of Philadelphia.
Davis, Daniel. 1762-1835.   91-02
    U.S. Att'y. Maine 1796-1801; Sol. Gen'l., Mass.
    1800-32.
Davis, Ignatius.   98-18
    Of Maryland.
Davis, John. 1774-1854.   98-51, 05-15, 05-32, 06-14, 08-48
    English author, traveller.
Davis, Matthew L. 1773-1850.   06-20, 07-24, 10-19
    Politician, of New York.

Fleming, Francis A.   -1793.   92-07
   Catholic writer.
Folwell, Richard.   -1814.   97-58, 98-64
   Philadelphia printer.
Ford, Timothy. 1762-1830.   92-13, 94-06
   Lawyer, legislature, S. Carolina.
Forrest, Michael.   97-41
   Of Philadelphia.
Foster, Abiel. 1735-1806.   91-19
   Clergyman, judge, Congressman, of N.H.
Fox, Henry R. V., Baron Holland. 1773-1840.   06-19
   English statesman, author.
Fox, William.   91-04, 91-15, 92-01, 92-03, 92-34
   English writer.
Franklin, Benjamin. 1706-1790.   90-10
   Statesman, philosopher, printer, scientist.
Franklin, William Temple.   -1823.   91-01
   Grandson, Secretary, Benjamin Franklin; agent
   of Robert Morris.
Fraser, Donald. fl. 1797-1802.   97-52, 98-55, 99-32
   Educator, of N.Y.
Freeman, James. 1759-1835.   93-29, 96-71, 02-10
   Clergyman, of Boston.
Freneau, Philip. 1752-1832.   96-60, 99-26
   Poet, newspaper editor.
Froeligh, Solomon. 1750-1827.   94-30
   Clergyman, N.Y. and N.J.

Gadsden, Christopher. 1723-1805.   97-20
   Of S. Car.; member, Continental Congress.
Gallatin, Albert. 1761-1849.   97-19, 02-02, 08-42
   Legislature, Pa., 1790-93; Cong. 1795-1801;
   Sec'y. Treas. 1801-13.
Gardiner, John S. J. 1765-1830.   95-41, 98-58
   Clergyman, Boston, 1792-1830.
Gardner, John.   96-16
   Of Boston, classical scholar.
Gaston, William. 1778-1844.   08-03
   N. Car. lawyer, judge, Congressman, 1813-15.
Genet, Edmond Charles. 1765-1834.   93-15, 93-19, 08-13, 08-31
   French Minister, 1793-94.

Hodgdon, Moses. 1774-1840.   06-07
   Lawyer, of New Hampshire.
Hodgkinson, John (?).   94-16
Holden, Oliver. 1765-1831.   89-11, 00-50
   Psalmist and composer, of Mass.
Holmes, Abiel. 1763-1837.   04-32
   Clergyman, historian, of Cambridge, Mass.
Honeywood, St. John. 1763-1798.   96-45, 96-46, 97-40, 00-39
   Artist, poet, of New York.
Hopkins, Joseph R.   04-27
   Lawyer, poet, of Philadelphia.
Hopkins, Lemuel. 1750-1801.   95-13, 95-16, 95-34, 96-27, 96-28,
   Poet of Connecticut.   96-76, 97-22, 98-28, 99-25, 99-36, 07-07
Hopkins, Samuel M. 1772-1837.   05-18
   Lawyer, Congressman from N.Y., 1813-15.
Hopkinson, Joseph. 1770-1842.   96-20, 98-29, 98-53, 98-71, 99-04,
   Lawyer, Congressman, judge, of Phila.   99-49, 09-12
Horry, Charles L. P.   97-21
   Englishman.
Houldbrooke,   92-29
   Scottish author.
Humphrey, Asa.   04-42
Humphreys, Daniel. 1740-1827.   96-11, 96-41, 02-22
   Of Portsmouth, N.H.
Humphreys, David. 1752-1818.   95-04
   Aide to Washington; diplomat; of Connecticut.
Hunn, John S.   06-30
   Conveyancer, notary, of N.Y.C.
Hunter, William. 1774-1849.   03-25
   Legislature, R.I., 1799-1812; U.S. Senator,
   1812-21.

Ingersoll, Charles J. 1782-1862.   10-16
   Lawyer, Congressman, of Philadelphia.
Innes, William.   90-25, 92-18
   English merchant.
Ives, Levi. 1750-1826.   03-31
   Physician, of New Haven.

Jackson, Andrew. 1767-1845.   01-11
   Seventh President.

Jackson, James. 1757-1806.   95-27
    Congressman from Ga., 1789-91; Senator, 1793-
    95; 1801-06; Governor, Ga., 1798-1801.
Jackson, John Mills.   09-33
    English political writer.
James, Joseph.   00-57
Jacquemart, N. Francois. 1735-1799.   90-19
    French writer.
Jefferson, Thomas. 1743-1826.   97-56
    Third President.
Jenks, William. 1778-1866.   08-33
    Clergyman, of Bath, Me. and Boston.
Johnson, Paul R. fl. 1800-1805.   02-21
    N.Y.C. printer.
Johnson, William. 1771-1834.   99-30
    Legislature, S.C., 1794-98; Judge, 1798-1804;
    U.S. Sup. Ct., 1804-34.
Jones, Absalom. 1746-1818.   94-21
    Black clergyman, of Philadelphia.
Jones, Calvin. 1775-1846.   07-03
    Physician, general, of N. Car.
Jones, Gabriel. 1724-1806.   03-29
    Lawyer, executer of Lord Fairfax, of Va.
Judd, William.   -1804.   04-50
    Connecticut justice, Republican.

Kelly, Alexander.   08-43
Kent, James. 1763-1847.   95-51
    Legislature, N.Y., Prof. of law, judge.
King, Nicholas.   07-01
    Mapmaker.
King, Rufus. 1755-1827.   06-06, 07-21, 08-29
    Senator from N.Y., 1789-96; Minister to
    England, 1796-1803.
Kinloch, Francis. 1755-1826.   00-25
    Legislature, South Carolina.
Knapp, Samuel L. 1783-1838.   02-18
    Lawyer, author of Boston and New York.
Knight, Dr. John.   -1838.   99-29
    Indian captive—see Vail 684.
Knox, Henry. 1750-1806.   90-21
    General; Sec'y. of War, 1789-94.

Knox, Samuel. 1756-1832.   00-62, 03-11
    Clergyman and educator, of Maryland.
Knox, Vicesimus. 1752-1821.   95-46, 99-43
    Editor, of London, England.

Lacock, Abner. 1770-1837.   07-17
    Legislature, Pa.; Representative from Pa.,
    1811-13; Senator, 1813-19.
Ladd,   fl. 1804.   04-04
Ladd, William. 1778-1841.   04-28
    Celebrated peace advocate.
La Roche, Sophie von. 1731-1807.   03-36
    German novelist.
La Rochefoucauld-Liancourt, Duc de.   96-22, 96-43, 99-15, 00-15
    French traveller in U.S.
Law, Thomas.   04-37
Lawrence, Jonathan (Sr.).   89-22
    N.Y. State Senator, 1773-83.
Leach, James.   95-33
Lear, Tobias. 1762-1816.   93-23, 94-25
    Secretary to Washington; diplomat, 1801-12.
Leavenworth, Mark. 1752-1812.   92-09
    Merchant, of Connecticut.
Lee, Charles. 1758-1815.   98-13, 98-56
    Legislature, Va.; U.S. Att'y. Gen'l. 1795-1801.
Lee, Henry. 1756-1818.   99-03, 99-07, 99-34, 00-27, 09-13
    Legislature, Va., 1789-91; Gov.,
    Va., 1792-95; Cong. from Va., 1799-1801.
Legal, G.   98-49
Leib, Michael. 1760-1822.   02-26, 08-01
    Cong. from Pa., 1798-1806; Senator, 1808-14.
Leigh, Benjamin Watkins. 1781-1849.   08-05
    Lawyer, Va.; U.S. Senator, 1834-36.
Leland, John. 1754-1841.   92-17, 93-14, 94-14, 94-37, 97-23, 06-41
    Clergyman, Va. and Mass.
Leonard, Daniel. 1740-1829.   92-33
    In U.S. to 1776; Chief Justice, Bermuda, 1782-1806.
Lesur, Charles Louis. 1770-1849.   10-21
    French publicist.
Letherbusy, Peregrine.   00-01
Lewis, William. 1751-1819.   90-14
    Lawyer, of Philadelphia.

Lincoln, Benjamin. 1733-1810.   93-09
  General, of Mass.; Indian Comm'r., 1789, 1793.
Lincoln, Levi. 1749-1820.   02-13, 02-20
  Legislature, Mass., 1796; Cong., 1801; U.S.
  Att'y. Gen'l., 1801-04.
Linn, William. 1752-1808.   00-51
  Clergyman, Pa. and N.Y.
Lislet, Louis C. E. Moreau de. 1767-1832.   07-09, 09-14
  Lawyer, of New Orleans.
Livingston, Edward. 1764-1836.   04-33, 04-36, 07-12, 09-25
  Congressman from N.Y., 1795-1801; U.S.
  Att'y., 1801-03; New Orleans, 1803-
Livingston, Henry Brockholst. 1757-1823.   94-09
  Judge, N.Y., 1802-06; U.S. Sup. Ct., 1807-
Livingston, Robert R. 1746-1813.   95-17
  Chancellor, N.Y., 1777-1801; French Mission,
  1801-04.
Livingston, William. 1723-1790.   89-07
  Lawyer, Governor of New Jersey.
Lloyd, Thomas.   99-42
  Stenographer, bookseller, of Philadelphia.
Locke, Joseph.   03-28
Logan, George. 1753-1821.   91-10, 92-15, 93-11, 93-17
  Legislature, Pa.; U.S. Senator, 1801-07.
Lovell, James. 1737-1814.   06-21
  Boston Collector, 1788-89; Naval officer, 1790-1814.
Lovett, John. 1761-1818.   00-60
  Legislature, N.Y. 1800-01; Cong. from N.Y., 1813-17.
Low, Samuel. 1765-   89-10, 89-14
  Poet, of New York.
Lowell, John. 1769-1840.   97-07, 98-23, 07-21, 08-46, 09-06, 09-08,
  Lawyer, writer, of Boston.   09-16, 09-27, 09-30, 10-01, 10-07,
                                                   10-08, 10-23, 10-31
Lyon, James.   01-24
  Editor, publisher, N.Y., Vt., Richmond, Va.,
  and D.C.

Macarty,   92-05
  Captain (?)
Macdonald, Thomas.   00-08
  English Commissioner under Jay Treaty.

Prince, Oliver Hillhouse. 1787-1837.   07-14
  Senator from Georgia 1828-29.
Puglia, Santiago Felipe. 1760- .   96-13, 96-52, 97-17, 99-37
  Came to U.S. 1790; foreign language
  teacher, Philadelphia.
Purcell, Henry.   -1802.   95-48
  Clergyman, of South Carolina.
Pye, Henry James. 1745-1813.   95-14
  English poet laureate.

Quincy, Josiah. 1772-1864.   05-06
  Legislature, Mass., 1804; Cong., 1805-12;
  Pres. of Harvard.

Raithby, John. 1766-1826.   06-38
  English lawyer, legal writer.
Ramsey, David. 1749-1815.   89-05, 91-12, 92-13
  Physician; So. Car. legislature.
Ranby, John. 1743-1820.   90-08, 91-11
  English pamphleteer.
Randolph, Edmund Jennings. 1753-1813.   94-13, 95-50, 96-01,
  Att'y. Gen'l., 1789-94; Sec'y. State,   96-53
  1794-95.
Randolph, John. 1773-1823.   05-20
  Congressman from Va., 1800-13.
Read, Jacob. 1752-1816.   98-61
  U.S. Senator, 1795-1801; judge of Charleston.
Read, John, Jr. 1769-1854.   98-48
  Legislature, Pa.; Agent, Jay Treaty, 1799-1809.
Reed, William. 1777-1837.   05-03
  Merchant, of Marblehead, Mass.
Reeve, Tapping. 1744-1823.   06-35
  Law instructor, Conn.; Judge, 1798-1814.
Relf, Samuel. 1776-1823.   96-57
  Philadelphia newspaper publisher.
Rhees, Morgan J. 1760-1804.   98-38
  Clergyman, land developer, of Penna.
Rice, David. 1733-1816.   92-32
  Clergyman, Kentucky.
Richards, George H.   -1814.   89-13, 93-07, 00-29
  Author, of Boston, Portsmouth, New London.

Tilghman, William. 1756-1827.   03-07
    Chief Justice Penna. Supreme Court.
Toulmin, Harry. 1767-1823.   92-10, 92-35
    Sec'y. Kentucky, 1796-1804; U.S. Judge,
    Mississippi, 1804.
Tracy, Uriah. 1755-1807.   98-56, 98-62
    Legislature, Conn., 1788-1793; Congress,
    1793-1796; U.S. Senate, 1796-1807.
Treziulney,   96-36, 97-29
    Printer, Phila.; employee of Wm. Duane.
Trimble, James.   08-12
Trumbull, Benjamin. 1735-1820.   98-06
    Clergyman, historian, of Connecticut.
Trumbull, Henry.   10-14
Trumbull, John. 1750-1831.   09-10
    Poet, jurist, of Connecticut.
Tucker, George. 1775-1861.   01-12, 03-19, 04-44
    Professor, Congressman from Va.,
    1819-1825.
Tucker, St. George. 1752-1828.   95-08, 95-29, 96-19, 96-60, 96-64,
    Law professor, judge, of Virginia.   99-27, 01-12, 03-28
Tudor, William. 1750-1819.   06-08
    Lawyer, legislator, of Boston.
Turner, George. fl. 1796-1817.   07-35
    Judge, Northwest Territory.
Tyler, Royall. 1757-1826.   90-07, 97-02, 01-19
    Playwright, novelist, jurist, of Vermont.

Van Horne, David. 1746-1801.   98-34
Van Ness, William Peter. 1778-1826.   95-01, 03-13, 04-08, 04-18,
    Lawyer, of New York.   04-25, 06-20, 07-24, 10-19
Van Pradelles, Capt. Benjamin.   92-24
    Of Flanders; land agent.
Van Vechten, Teunis A. fl. 1806.   06-32
    Of Albany.
Vaughan, Benjamin. 1751-1835.   10-31
    English M.P. In Maine, 1796-
Vaughan, John. 1775-1807.   00-65

Wagner, Jacob.   03-01, 04-01, 04-03
    State Department Chief Clerk.

LIST OF PSEUDONYMS

B. See Bordley under Author Index.
B., S. (Blodget)   08-16
A Bostonian (Lowell)   09-16, 10-07
The British Spy (Wirt)   03-19, 04-12, 05-21
Brown, Alexander Campbell (Leavenworth)   92-09
Brutus, Lucius Junius (Cranch)   01-09
Brutus, Marcus (Pollard)   00-52
Bystander (Harper)   00-10

Caius (Pinkney)   00-26
Callender, Tom   02-19
Camillus (Duane)   03-22
Camillus (Forrest)   97-41
Camillus (Hamilton)   95-12, 97-41
Cato (Livingston)   95-17
Caustic, Christopher (Fessenden)   05-12, 06-10
Chatham (Webster)   03-04
A Citizen (Findley)   94-31
A Citizen (Ogden)   99-41
A Citizen (Rush)   09-26
A Citizen (Smith)   04-06
A Citizen of Boston (Richards)   93-07
A Citizen of Connecticut (Beers)   91-03
A Citizen of Massachusetts (Bowdoin)   97-38
A Citizen of Massachusetts (Holden)   00-50
A Citizen of Massachusetts (Nichols)   02-11
A Citizen of Massachusetts (Sullivan)   92-21
A Citizen of New England (Lowell)   97-07
A Citizen of New York (Cheetham)   00-06, 02-23
A Citizen of New York (Genet)   08-13, 08-31
A Citizen of Pennsylvania (Gallatin)   97-19
A Citizen of Pennsylvania (Rush)   90-13
A Citizen of Philadelphia (Murdock)   98-52
A Citizen of Philadelphia (Webster)   89-06, 90-09, 90-22, 91-05, 91-20
A Citizen of South Carolina (Ford)   92-13
A Citizen of South Carolina (Ramsay)   91-12
A Citizen of South Carolina (Smith)   95-07, 99-08
A Citizen of That State (Jackson)   95-27
A Citizen of These States (Ogden)   00-33
A Citizen of the United States (Coxe)   89-08
A Citizen of the United States (Tucker)   96-64

A Citizen of the United States (Wood)   94-35
A Citizen of this State (Evans)   98-05
A Citizen of Trenton (Chauvet)   98-12
A Citizen of Westmoreland County (Lee)   99-34
A Citizen of Williamsburg (Tucker)   95-29
Un Citoyen adoptif (Bonnet)   95-43
Citoyen de Novion (Sullivan)   95-02
Columbus (Tucker) or (Wood)   95-08, 96-64, 99-27
Columella (Moore)   06-17
Connecticutensis (Daggett)   00-58
Constantia (Murray)   98-27
Coriolanus (Smith)   03-30
Cornelius (Bentley)   99-22
Crabshaw, Timothy (Prince)   07-14
Crassus, Lucius (Hamilton)   02-12
Curtius (Taylor)   04-21
Curtius (Thomson)   98-37
Curtius (Webster)   95-51

D., B. (Baudry)   02-34
Decius (Courtenay)   08-35
Decius (Montgomery)   89-03
Decius (Randolph)   05-20
A Delaware Waggoner (Nelson)   00-31
Democritus (Brackenridge)   02-31
Detector, Daniel (Henderson)   96-06
Dobbins, Peter (Fessenden)   07-25
Dwight, Jasper, of Vermont (Duane)   96-36, 97-29

Epaminondas (Woodward)   01-05, 01-08, 06-42
Un Espanol, en Philadelphia (Yrujo)   99-37
An European (La Rochefoucauld-Liancourt)   96-43
Un Europeen (La Rochefoucauld-Liancourt)   96-22, 99-15, 00-15

F., J. (Freeman)   93-29
Fabius (Dickinson)   97-27
A Farmer (Lincoln)   02-13, 02-20
A Farmer (Logan)   91-10, 92-15
A Farmer (Whipple)   02-17
A Farmer of Windham County (Phelps)   08-37
A Federal Republican (Desaussure)   00-02

A Fellow-Sufferer (Park)   08-02
Un Francais voyageur (Moreau)   98-25
Franklin (Dallas)   95-26
A Friend to common honesty (Davis)   10-04
A Friend to liberty (Bailey)   02-06
A Friend to National Industry (Blodget)   05-14
A Friend to peace (Lowell)   08-46
A Friend to Political Equality (Carey)   96-44
A Friend to real religion (Knox)   00-62
A Friend to Regular Government (Callender)   96-17
A Friend to the constitution (Carroll)   02-15
A Friend to the Public Welfare (Daggett)   05-31
A Friend to truth and justice (Armstrong)   06-13

G., J. (Greenleaf)   94-05
A Genevan (Chauvet)   98-35
A Gentleman (Ogden)   95-25
A Gentleman (Williamson)   99-14
A Gentleman formerly of Boston (Church)   89-02
A Gentleman from South Carolina (Devot)   07-15
A Gentleman in America (Cooper)   94-12, 98-24
A Gentleman in Philadelphia (Cooper)   94-34
A Gentleman lately returned (Hodgkinson)   94-16
A Gentleman of Connecticut (Hopkins)   95-13, 96-76
A Gentleman of New York (Fraser)   99-32
A Gentleman of North Carolina (Van Ness)   04-08
A Gentleman of Philadelphia (Bordley)   03-15
A Gentleman of Portsmouth (Sewall)   98-70
A Gentleman of the bar (Bland)   08-11
A Gentleman of the bar (Tatham)   94-29
A Gentleman of the profession (Hodgdon)   06-07
Germanicus (Randolph)   94-13
Greene (Coxe)   00-56
Grievous, Peter, Junr. (Hopkinson)   96-20
Grotius (Clinton)   00-63

H., S. J. (Honeywood)   96-45
Hampden (Daggett) or (Webster)   08-32
Hancock (Russell)   08-49, 09-35
Hedgehog, Henry (Carey)   97-06
Helvidius (Madison)   96-34

Hermes (Rodney)   91-13
Historicus (Sampson)   02-29, 04-45
Holdfast, Simon (Daggett)   03-14
Hortensius (Ford)   92-13
Hortensius (Hay)   99-19, 03-10
A Householder (Hopkins)   05-18

An Impartial Citizen (Sullivan)   01-07
Impartialis (Plumer)   04-05
Inchiquin (Ingersoll)   10-16
Independent American (Morford)   06-18
An Inhabitant (Williams)   90-05
An Inhabitant of Boston (Newell)   06-09
An Inquirer (Tucker)   03-19

J., A. (Jones)   94-21
Judd, William (Bishop)   04-50
Juriscola (Coxe)   07-10
Juvenal, Horatio (Alsop)   90-24, 90-28

A Kentuckian (Winterfield)   07-23

Laco (Higginson)   89-24
A Lady (Ritson)   09-24
A Layman (Brown)   00-11
A Layman (Fisher)   96-65
A Layman (Williams)   94-02
The Lay Preacher (Dennie)   96-33
Leonidas (Cheetham)   01-18
A Lover of the Truth (Haynes)   93-31
Lycurgus (Wood)   94-35
Lysander (Cheetham)   02-04
Lysander (Wills)   04-18

Manlius (Gore)   94-19
Marcus (Van Ness)   06-20, 07-24, 10-19
Marcus (Wolcott)   04-11
Martin, John Paul (Bishop)   91-21
Massachusettensis (Leonard)   92-33
A Member of the House of Representatives (Dennis)   98-04
A Member of the House of Representatives (Desaussure)   99-30

A Member of the Old Congress (Beresford)	93-28, 97-59
Mercer (Cheetham)	03-17
A Merchant (Bird)	94-36
Munro, Robert (Williamson)	04-22
A Native American (Wilmer)	09-20
A Native of Charleston (Smith)	08-30
A Native of Pennsylvania (Sansom)	05-19
A Native of Scotland (Bruce)	01-14
A New England Farmer (Lowell)	98-23
A New Jersey Farmer (Snowden)	95-09
Nips, Jack (Leland)	92-17, 93-14, 94-37
Numa (Colvin)	10-18
Observator (Blodget)	01-22
An Officer of the militia (Van Horne)	98-34
Officer under that general (Biggs)	08-26
An old fashioned clergyman (Bowden)	09-22
An Old Member of Parliament (Ranby)	90-08
An Old Statesman (Williams)	91-09
An Old Whig (Cheetham)	10-22
An Old Whig (Webster)	05-07
One of the American People (Sargent)	01-15
One of their Fellow Citizens (Davis)	91-02
Pacificus (Hamilton)	96-35
Pasquin, Anthony (Williams)	04-26
Patrioticus (Russell)	07-19, 07-30
Pepper Box, Peter (Fessenden)	09-23
Petronius, Pasquin (Alsop)	07-07
Philaenus, Junius (Johnson)	02-21
Philalathes (Montfort)	89-20
Philanthropos (Ladd)	04-28
Philanthropos (Rice)	92-32
Philo-Cato (Davis)	10-19
Philodemus (Nelson)	98-22
Phocion (Desaussure)	95-28
Phocion (Hartley)	89-09
Phocion (Smith)	96-58, 96-59, 06-05, 06-28
Pindar, Jonathan (Tucker)	96-60
Plain Sense (Sands)	92-26

<tr><td>The Stranger (Story)</td><td>95-30</td></tr>
<tr><td>Sylvestris (Tucker)</td><td>03-28</td></tr>
</table>

T., W. (Thornton)	04-43
Tacitus (Evans)	02-28
Timoleon (Wortman)	00-54
Telltruth, Timothy (Carey)	99-10
Touchstone, Geoffrey (Carey)	96-29, 98-31
Two Gentlemen of law knowledge (Turner)	07-35

Union (Murray)	96-59

Veritas (Binns)	07-28
Veritas (Grymes)	03-20
Verus (Burges)	90-15
Verus (de Onis)	10-26
Verus (Yrujo)	97-28, 97-30
Vindex (Allison)	93-05
Vindex (Eden)	07-20
Vindex (Paine)	93-25
A Virginian born and bred (Hay)	96-63
Virginiensis (Lee)	98-13

Warren (Cheetham)	02-05
A West Indian merchant (Innes)	90-25, 92-18
Wilson, Jasper (Currie)	93-16

X (Tucker)	04-44

A Yankee Farmer (Lowell)	07-21
A Young Gentleman of Philadelphia (Hopkins)	04-27
A Young German (Behrens)	04-47
A Youth of Thirteen (Bryant)	08-18